Whose Business?

*An analysis of the failure of British
business schools and a radical proposal
for their privatisation*

BRIAN GRIFFITHS

*Dean, City University Business School &
Professor of Banking and International Finance*

and

HUGH MURRAY

*Academic Sub-Dean, City University Business School &
Midland Bank Professor of Export Management
and International Business*

Published by

THE INSTITUTE OF ECONOMIC AFFAIRS

1985

First published in June 1985

by

THE INSTITUTE OF ECONOMIC AFFAIRS
2 Lord North Street, Westminster,
London SW1P 3LB

© THE INSTITUTE OF ECONOMIC AFFAIRS 1985

ISSN 0073-2818
ISBN 0-255 36182-3

Printed in Great Britain by
GORON PRO-PRINT CO LTD
6 Marlborough Road, Churchill Industrial Estate, Lancing, W. Sussex
Text set in 'Monotype' Baskerville

CONTENTS

[3]

[4]

[5]

TABLES

[6]

PREFACE

The *Hobart Papers* are intended to contribute a stream of authoritative, independent and lucid analyses to the understanding and application of economics to private and government activity. The characteristic theme has been the optimum use of scarce resources and the extent to which it can best be achieved in markets within an appropriate framework of laws and institutions or, where markets cannot work, in other ways. Since in the real world the alternative to the market is the state, and both are imperfect, the choice between them effectively turns on a judgement of the comparative consequences of 'market failure' and 'governmental failure'.

The subject of Hobart Paper 102 is an activity which, in Britain, is largely funded and extensively controlled by government but whose ostensible purpose is to equip its 'customers' with skills that enable them to excel in the market-place—namely, formal business education. *A priori*, we might be sceptical that such an arrangement would produce the desired results. Activities financed and controlled by government not infrequently develop an ethos which is risk-averse and non-entrepreneurial. Why should we expect that, within such a setting, businessmen and would-be businessmen can be imbued with the aptitudes and values which make for success in the uncertain and risky environment of the market-place?

The short answer, say the authors, is that we should *not* expect it. And from their vantage point within the present system as, respectively, Dean and Academic Sub-Dean of City University Business School, Professors Brian Griffiths and Hugh Murray argue that postgraduate business education in Britain must on the whole be judged a failure. Twenty-two years after the Franks Report formally launched the business school concept here, not only have our schools failed to produce the target numbers of business graduates anticipated at that time; worse, the relevance of much teaching is constantly questioned by industry and commerce. Moreover, complaints that the schools are remote from business, that their curricula are too academic in emphasis, and that too few of their full-time staff have substantial business experience are not new; such criticisms have been expressed at regular intervals since the schools were established in the mid-1960s.

Professors Griffiths and Murray believe that postgraduate business education *can* make an important contribution to improving the efficiency of corporate management. They do not, however, believe that the potential will be realised under the present business school system. That system, they argue, is flawed in two fundamental respects. First, having been captured by the university system, British business schools suffer from many of the inefficiencies and inflexibilities which characterise the university education cartel in this country. Secondly, the heavy dependence of the business schools on public funding drives a wedge between producer and consumer with the result that, as producers, business schools are not sufficiently responsive to the requirements of their consumers, that is, students and companies. Although there is considerable diversity among British business schools, all but Cranfield share the following characteristics: they are attached to British universities and abide by the University Grants Committee cartel in the minimum fees they charge students; the salaries of their staff are fixed on the agreed UGC scale and life tenure is the standard expectation of most staff; their ethos is indistinguishable from that of a university; and none of them has less than 50 per cent public funding (80 per cent of the total full-time academic staff at British schools are financed by the taxpayer).

The consequence, maintain Professors Griffiths and Murray, is that risk-taking is being taught in and by a risk-averse culture more conducive to leisurely and scholarly reflection than to equipping students with practical management skills. Whilst those who teach business 'shelter in a protected and secure part of the public sector, those who practise business are exposed to a highly uncertain and changing environment'. Thus the interests of business school staff, their research focus, and the emphasis of the curricula they teach all tend to reflect the internal environment of the business school rather than the external environment of business in the market-place.

What is required, argue the authors, to make business schools more responsive to the needs of their business customers is a different system of property rights which will ensure that their activities are guided by the discipline of the market. To that end, they outline a radical plan for reforming postgraduate business education. The business schools would be separated from the universities and established as autonomous legal entities. Public funding of their activities would be phased out over a period of years after which they would be expected to maintain themselves by selling their services in the market-place and attracting private endowments. They would compete on the fees they charged students and on the salaries and terms of employment they offered their staffs so that, to the extent tenure survived, it would be guaranteed not by the taxpayer but by the continuing success of a school. Finally, they would be managed by their boards of directors and partners, with strong business participation.

The authors believe that their reform plan would have several beneficial results. It would save the taxpayer around £10 million a year; it would improve the internal management of the business schools, ensuring that product mix, quality, design and price were attractive; it would open the way for a general rise in staff salaries, though with wider variations than at present; it would improve the quality of teaching and other services received by students; it would lead to a significant increase in the number of applicants for business degree courses; it would set an example for the de-regulation of all postgraduate vocational training in British universities; it would give business a joint role in determining the strategy of business schools and the allocation of resources within them, rather than being—as now—a largely passive recipient of business school offerings; and it would encourage the integration between business and business school activity at all levels within different sectors of commercial and industrial specialisation.

Such results would be major achievements, undoubtedly worth striving for. Although the constitution of the Institute obliges it to dissociate its Trustees, Directors and Advisers from the authors' analyses and conclusions, it offers their *Hobart Paper* as a radical, vigorous and, indeed, courageous initiative from within the present business school system. Its aim is to focus wider public attention on what is wrong with that system and on the reforms required for business schools to live up to the expectations they aroused 20 years ago.

May 1985   MARTIN WASSELL

THE AUTHORS

BRIAN GRIFFITHS was born in Swansea, S. Wales, in 1941 and educated at Dynevor Grammar School and the London School of Economics. He taught at the LSE, specialising in the field of money and finance, from 1965 until the end of 1976, when he was appointed Professor of Banking and International Finance and Director of the Centre for Banking and International Finance at the City University, London. Since 1982 he has been Dean of the City University Business School. In 1984 he was appointed Gresham Professor of Ethics at Gresham College.

Professor Griffiths has written and broadcast extensively on money and finance and has for some years acted as consultant to various City firms. Since March 1984 he has been a Director of the Bank of England. He has written variously for the Institute of Economic Affairs, including a previous *Hobart Paper* (No. 51) on *Competition in Banking* (1970). He has also published *Inflation: the Price of Prosperity* (1976), *Morality and the Market Place* (1982), and *The Creation of Wealth* (1984).

HUGH MURRAY, who was born in Birkenhead in 1931 and educated at Park High School, Birkenhead, and the University of Liverpool, is Midland Bank Professor of Export Management and International Business, and Academic Sub-Dean at the City University Business School. He is also Gresham Professor of Management at Gresham College and a visiting professor at the Open University.

Professor Murray has held appointments in marketing at The Chinese University of Hong Kong and The London Business School, where he directed the London Executive Programme, and has taught on a regular basis at business schools in Germany, Portugal and Japan. Prior to his academic career, he worked in management positions for Attwoods Marketing, the Newcastle Chronicle and Journal Ltd, and the Liverpool

Daily Post and Echo Ltd., and as Marketing Director for Letraset and Managing Director for Transprint Ltd.

He has published a number of articles in academic journals on the subject of international business.

ACKNOWLEDGEMENTS

We would like to acknowledge our gratitude to Professors Michael Beenstock, Andrew Ehrenberg, Mr J. P. Martin-Bates and others who read an earlier draft of this *Hobart Paper* and who made useful comments. They are in no way responsible for the views expressed here.

We are also extremely grateful to Miss Rachel Steare who provided first-class research assistance and secretarial support.

B.G.
H.M.

I. INTRODUCTION

The theme of this *Hobart Paper* is that British business schools are in need of radical reform. Our concern is not with the shortcomings of individual schools but with the British system of postgraduate business education as a whole. Our *Paper* is a contribution to the national debate on this issue and aims to bring business schools closer to business so that they may serve the nation more effectively.

Failed expectations

Although schools such as the Administrative Staff College at Henley and the Cranfield School of Management have long run courses in business administration, the business school concept was formally launched in the UK by the Franks Report of 1963, which built on the Robbins Report of the same year. When the establishment of business schools was originally proposed by Robbins and Franks, high expectations were held for them. They were to have 'a scale, range of activities and quality' which would 'produce major effects in business life'.[1] Reference was made to the possibility of creating a British version of the Harvard Business School. It was firmly expected that they would turn out around 2,000 Masters of Business Administration (MBAs) a year, of which the newly-established schools of London and Manchester would each turn out 200.[2]

Twenty years later, there are 28 business schools or departments of management in British universities (including Cranfield) which offer MBA degrees or an equivalent qualification. The system has hardly lived up to the expectations held out for it in the Franks Report. The total number of British students engaged in full-time postgraduate business and management studies has increased from about 1,355 in 1972/73 to about 1,530 in 1982/83—a rise of approximately 13 per cent over 10 years. But since some are registered for

[1] Report by The Rt. Hon. Lord Franks, *British Business Schools*, British Institute of Management, 1963, para. 7.

[2] *Ibid.*, para. 38.

[13]

other higher degrees, such as MPhils or PhDs, or are taking an MBA course over two years, the number of MBAs graduating each year is considerably lower and falls far short of the Franks target.[1] London and Manchester between them are producing just over one-half of what Franks expected of them. The total number of full-time postgraduates at the business schools in 1982/83 was 2,485, of whom 956 were overseas students.[2] While the high proportion of overseas students reflects the international attractiveness of British business schools, it makes no contribution to the problem Franks was trying to solve in proposing the establishment of business schools. To match the United States proportionately, British universities would have to produce around 15,000 business graduates a year.

Not only have the business schools failed to meet the target numbers expected by Franks, however; the relevance of what they are producing is also being questioned by industry and commerce. In a recent survey, *Masters of Business?*, undertaken by Harbridge House,[3] Kate Ascher acknowledged that it was dangerous to generalise about British industry's view of MBA courses or graduates because no single view appeared to exist, but reported a lack of favourable comment from industry and commerce about the MBA degree.

'. . . recent evidence indicates that acceptance of the MBA degree in Britain has not been as whole-hearted as in other countries. A number of studies published in 1983 show that many companies are not convinced that the MBA programmes have succeeded in making a significant contribution to either their individual

[1] These figures refer to the number of home postgraduate students on full-time and sandwich courses (Table 4, Annex G, in *A strategy for higher education into the 1990s*, The University Grants Committee's Advice, September 1984, p. 81). The data available do not indicate how many of these home postgraduate students were on MBA courses and they include postgraduate students on other than MBA courses. It is possible to exclude from the figures students on two-year MBA courses at the London and Manchester Business Schools, by subtracting the number of new home entrants to these two schools from the total of home postgraduate students (Table 17 in *Statistics of Education: Vol. 6—Universities 1972*, published by the University Grants Committee, 1972, and Table 15 in *University Statistics 1982-83: volume one—Students and Staff*, published by the Universities' Statistical Record, 1983). The number of British postgraduate students graduating from UK business schools in 1972-73 was 1,354 minus 142=1,212; the number in 1982-83 was 1,529 minus 172=1,357.

[2] *University Statistics 1982-83: volume one—Students and Staff*, ibid., Table 6.

[3] Harbridge House Europe is a subsidiary of Harbridge House Inc., which was founded in 1950 by a group of professors from the Harvard Business School. It is engaged in both management education and management consultancy. Kate Ascher is a consultant for Harbridge House Europe.

Whose Business?

BRIAN GRIFFITHS and HUGH MURRAY

1. Rigorous postgraduate and post-experience business education has a major contribution to make to the creation of wealth.

2. The UK's present system of business schools suffers from crucial weaknesses: it is too academic, excessively restricted, remote from business, and buttressed by lifetime security of tenure.

3. These weaknesses stem from the original, flawed conception of business schools as substantially publicly-funded and part of the university 'industry'—which suffers from being organised as a classic cartel.

4. Radical reform is required which should remove postgraduate business education into distinct business schools with the status of independent legal entities outside the public sector.

5. Over a three-year period, all postgraduate business school activity should cease to be government-funded and should be financed by fees and endowments.

6. Salaries and terms and conditions of employment at the private postgraduate business schools should be market-determined; the schools should be managed by their boards of directors or partners.

7. Because fundamental research is a public good which yields benefits not confined to its initiators, it should continue to be eligible for grants from the Economic and Social Research Council.

8. Students, business, business schools and the taxpayer would all benefit from these reforms.

9. Students would enjoy higher standards of teaching and service; the business schools would have a larger market and clearer rationale; business would be more actively involved in the training process and better served; and government expenditure could be reduced.

10. Removing government controls and funding from business schools would provide a model for shifting all vocational postgraduate education into the competitive market so as to improve the quality and diversity of training and save the taxpayer even larger sums of money.

Hobart Paper 102 is published (price £2·50) by

THE INSTITUTE OF ECONOMIC AFFAIRS
2 Lord North Street, Westminster
London SW1P 3LB   Telephone: 01-799 3745

IEA PUBLICATIONS

Subscription Service

An annual subscription is the most convenient way to obtain our publications. Every title we produce in all our regular series will be sent to you immediately on publication and without further charge, representing a substantial saving.

Subscription rates*

Britain: £15.00 p.a. including postage.
£14.00 p.a. if paid by Banker's Order.
£10.00 p.a. teachers and students who pay *personally.*

Europe and South America: £20 or equivalent.

Other countries: Rates on application. In most countries subscriptions are handled by local agents.

*These rates are *not* available to companies or to institutions.

To: The Treasurer, Institute of Economic Affairs,
2 Lord North Street,
Westminster, London SW1P 3LB.

I should like to subscribe beginning ....
I enclose a cheque/postal order for:

☐ £15.00

☐ Please send me a Banker's Order form

☐ Please send me an Invoice

☐ £10.00 [I am a teacher/student at...................................]

Name ....

Address ....

....

Signed .... Date ....

HP102

or collective welfare. These studies also suggest that while certain sectors of industry have maintained a fairly constant intake of MBAs, other sectors have engaged in only sporadic recruitment.

'Business graduates, specifically MBAs, are universally aware of the lukewarm attitude towards them on the part of British industry. The graduates' perceptions are first-hand and stem from disappointing contact with many potential employers. Some graduates have commented on their concern to the schools and there is evidence that a number of business schools are trying to combat the poor opinions of their courses and graduates which prevail in certain sectors of industry.'[1]

In another recent article on the subject (in a special Touche Ross publication on business schools worldwide) entitled 'Why have British business schools failed?', Kenneth Fleet, the City Editor of *The Times*, recalls the view of the chairman of one leading UK retail company:

'In management training we must go back to the drawing board. The present labyrinth of management education is stuffed with jargon and academic theory, much of it utterly unrelated to practical needs.'

Mr Fleet goes on to say:

'An extreme judgement, perhaps, but it does reflect disappointment among senior businessmen with the state of management education in British business schools. If today they were asked to dig into their companies' pockets to finance a new British business school, they would keep their arms folded firmly across their chests. I doubt whether many of them would offer even to lend a drawing board.'[2]

Harsh, perhaps, but criticisms such as these have not been confined to businessmen. John Treasure, former Dean of the City University Business School, has stated that business schools 'have become far too academic and remote',[3] and Tom Lupton, former Director of the Manchester Business School, believes that British business schools are 'a faulty design and in need of radical change'.[4]

[1] Kate Ascher, *Masters of Business?: the MBA and British industry*, Harbridge House, 1984, p. 1.

[2] Kenneth Fleet, 'Why have British business schools failed?', in *Touche Ross Report on Business Education*, Touche Ross, 1984, p. 5.

[3] John Treasure, quoted by Kenneth Fleet in *ibid.*, p. 9.

[4] Tom Lupton, quoted by Kenneth Fleet in *ibid.*, p. 9.

Most recently, in a survey undertaken by the British Institute of Management (BIM) entitled *Management development and training 1984: a review of current policy and practice*, Malcolm Peel[1] summed up the position thus:

'The MBA, whether from British or USA business schools, but especially the former, has not to this day gained wide acceptance in British industry. MBAs are seen as too theoretical, too mobile, far too highly priced and too disruptive to other managers.'[2]

The criticisms are not new

These criticisms do not indicate a recent deterioration in the relationships between business and business schools. They reflect something more serious. Similar doubts and comments have been expressed in as trenchant a manner ever since the business schools were set up in the mid-1960s.

In 1969, just two years after the first graduates appeared from London and Manchester, Alistair Mant,[3] in a study for the BIM, found that:

'A startling number of people, and especially senior executives, are quite sceptical of much of the post-experience management training available today.'[4]

Indeed, nearly 40 per cent of the chief executives surveyed were 'doubtful' or 'quite sceptical' about the impact of the *best* external courses for experienced managers. Mant went on to say that this scepticism was well-founded on several grounds: most management education programmes for experienced managers were traditional in form and content, little attention was paid to the problem of transmitting classroom learning to the workplace, and there was an absence of any coherent theory of experienced manager action or learning.[5]

Of business schools in particular, Mant's report made the following observations:

[1] Malcolm Peel is Programme Development Adviser to the Management Development Division of the BIM.

[2] Malcolm Peel, *Management development and training: a review of current policy and practice*, British Institute of Management, 1984, p. 16.

[3] Alistair Mant was seconded by IBM (UK) Ltd. to the BIM to conduct the survey. He was awarded the Bowie Medal by the BIM for his report.

[4] Alistair Mant, *The experienced manager: a major resource*, British Institute of Management, 1969, Section 1, para. 3.

[5] *Ibid.*, Section 1, para. 4.

'The university sector is also most closely wedded to the traditional academic reward system, which means, to put it brutally, that in terms of advancement, a published paper is worth a good deal more than an inspired, experienced manager.'

'In the university sector there seem to be constraints on the development of the new breed of teacher.'

'As yet, the university schools are hesitant about courses designed for institutional learning.'

'Members of other university centres have carried on highly successful (and profitable) institutional learning activities almost surreptitiously, recognising that the academic establishment is never entirely happy about teachers of business behaving like businessmen.'[1]

In 1970, Andrew Robertson, of the Science Policy Research Unit at the University of Sussex, wrote of business education:

'Everything in the garden is not idyllic. Hardly a week goes by without some major attack being launched in the press against business schools . . . One of the common complaints is of inapplicability of "academic" thinking . . .'.[2]

In the same year, Sir John Partridge, then President of the Confederation of British Industry (CBI) and Chairman of the Council of Industry for Management Education (CIME), wrote in *The Economist*: 'There is now a very wide gulf between what the British business schools want to do and what industry thinks they ought to do.'[3]

In the following year the BIM, along with the CIME, published another critical report entitled *Business school programmes: the requirements of British manufacturing industry* (also known as the Owen Report, 1971). The report summarised 'the current views and requirements of manufacturing industry on the subject of postgraduate and post-experience education at business schools'.[4] It was based on the experience of 53 large and medium-sized firms. The researchers were surprised by 'the strength and basic uniformity of view on major issues' and

[1] *Ibid.*, Section 3b, p. 25.

[2] Andrew Robertson, 'Business schools—is the backlash justified?', *Management Decision*, 1970, No. 4.

[3] Sir John Partridge, 'What's wrong with business education?', in *The Economist*, 21 November 1970.

[4] BIM, *Business school programmes: the requirements of British manufacturing industry* (The Owen Report), British Institute of Management, 1971, p. 4.

felt that their report was 'a true consensus of opinion among those surveyed'. It was devastating in its criticism of business schools: 'Most of the people we met were in varying degree, perplexed, worried or angry about postgraduate education.'[1] Employers were concerned about entry standards and felt that more attention should be given to 'the qualities which will be needed by the business graduate if he is to succeed in management'.[2]

Then, in 1972, just five years after the London and Manchester business schools were founded, Professor Walter Reid, now a distinguished professor at the London Business School, in a most incisive analysis, conceded that the specific criticisms of the schools from outsiders were valid—namely, that the schools were too academic in emphasis, that there were too few full-time staff with substantial business experience, and that communications and contact between the schools and business were inadequate. He recommended the removal of detailed control of business schools from the University Grants Committee, though not the ending of public funding.[3]

The criticisms continued throughout the 1970s. A 1976 survey by the Business Graduate Association, for example, concluded that:

'The typical business graduate's perception of what the business schools are trying to do is at some variance with what he thinks they ought to be doing. He considers, for instance, that business schools appear to be developing theoretical disciplines rather than the application of skills and techniques. He does not consider the schools should be doing this. In other words, our typical British business graduate, who has had several years of business experience before going to business school, considers that the business schools are too academically oriented. . . . Some business graduates . . . consider that the business schools are devoting too much effort to research at the expense of teaching.'[4]

A more recent survey by Peter Forrester,[5] published in 1984, claimed that this student perception has now changed: 'From

[1] *Ibid.*, p. 12.

[2] *Ibid.*, p. 5.

[3] Walter Reid, 'Rethinking the business schools', *Management Today*, June 1971.

[4] BGA, *Business graduates: some attitudes towards business schools, 1976*, A British Graduate Association Survey, 30 September 1976, p. 3a.

[5] Peter Forrester, CBE, was the Director of the Cranfield School of Management from its foundation in 1967 until 1982.

the standpoint of the business schools, the results of the survey are very encouraging.'[1] A detailed examination of the results of Forrester's survey, however, hardly seems to justify the author's rather sanguine conclusions. From the sample of managers interviewed, 48 per cent indicated that the contents of their MBA courses were either of 'no use' or of 'peripheral use' to them as managers. On individual topics taught, over 75 per cent of the responses indicated that courses in quantitative methods were also of 'no use' or 'peripheral'. By comparison, over 60 per cent rated the management of people as being of either 'much' or 'essential' use.[2] This evidence does not support Forrester's conclusion that 'the balance of syllabi are not far from the optimum'.[3] Nor does it warrant his claim that 'from the standpoint of the business schools the results of the survey are very encouraging'. Any business whose product line was rejected by 48 per cent of its customers would consider that it had grounds for concern rather than self-congratulation.

Do we need business schools at all?

The criticisms made by both industry and postgraduates are born of disappointment with what has been and is being offered by the schools. Both are seeking change in business schools, not their elimination. When they criticise the 'too academic' approach, they are not being anti-intellectual: they are demanding highly intellectual analysis, synthesis and exposition relevant to more effective management.

We live today in a world economy which has become increasingly competitive, in which Britain has been rapidly losing market share, both in exports of manufactured goods *and* services. For British companies to compete successfully with their counterparts from continental Europe, the United States and East Asia at a time of rapid technological and regulatory change, we as a nation require a culture much more favourable to enterprise, and businessmen who are thoroughly professional in their whole approach to enterprise and management.

We believe that business schools have a key part to play in

---

[1] Peter Forrester, *A study of the practical use of the MBA*, British Institute of Management, 1984, p. 4.

[2] *Ibid.*, pp. 8 and 9.

[3] *Ibid.*, p. 4.

this task. They can obviously teach a number of quite specific management techniques—such as accounting, corporate finance, budgetary control, taxation, business law, market research, product planning and pricing, organisational analysis and design, leadership skills and marketing techniques—which are the standard tools of modern business. In addition, they can teach when and why these tools are to be used, either singly or in combination, in order to solve the more general problems of policy and strategy. In this context, the use of case studies and business games are invaluable simulation devices, describing real business situations at moments of decision and crisis, requiring analysis, decision-making and the examination of alternative ways of implementing decisions, and taking into account the environment of a specific company.

Although the value of business schools has been recognised by their worldwide development over the past two decades, it would be wrong to overstate the case for them. To use an analogy: military staff colleges would never pretend to guarantee to produce a Montgomery, Wellington or Marlborough, but *can* guarantee a highly professional officer corps. In the same way, business schools can never be a substitute for the genius of a Cadbury, Nuffield or Boulton, but they *can* nevertheless produce highly professional and competent managers eager to start and develop companies which can penetrate world markets and create jobs at home.

We conclude that MBAs are clearly valued by companies, otherwise an MBA would not have a positive market value. At the same time, the present MBA curriculum is not ideal and business does have many legitimate criticisms of business schools. Finally, the total number of MBAs being produced in the UK is far fewer than Franks anticipated and is substantially fewer, proportionately, than in the USA.

The need for radical change

In this *Hobart Paper* we attempt to analyse the reasons for the relative lack of success of British business schools. Critical to our findings are:

(i) the cartelised nature of university education in the UK, which results in the inefficiencies and inflexibilities associated with any cartel and in which the business schools sit uneasily. There are few business schools in

the UK which are wholly satisfied with their organisational relationship with the rest of the university.

(ii) the public funding of business education, which drives
a wedge between producer and consumer with the
result that, as producers, business schools are not
sufficiently responsive to the needs of consumers.

Section II examines the origins and structure of British
business schools in terms of the climate of the early 1960s and
the Robbins and Franks Reports, noting in particular the way
in which the schools were captured by the university system.
Section III examines the reasons why business schools have not
lived up to their expectations, emphasising in particular that
business schools are part of a publicly-funded and government-
directed cartel. Section IV puts forward a radical six-point
plan for reform and discusses the problems of implementation,
while Section V considers the principal objections which are
likely to be made to our proposals. Section VI is concerned with
the way ahead academically, and the final Section summarises
our conclusions and sets out our recommendations.

Although we argue in this *Paper* for radical change, it is
important for us to emphasise that

(a) we see great value in business education for individuals
and companies and expanding opportunities for its development in the increasingly competitive, changing and
deregulated world economy in which we live;

(b) we know from first-hand experience that the intellectual
quality and motivation of students entering business
schools in the UK are very high;[1]

(c) a high-calibre research output is an important element
in any lively teaching institution; and

(d) we are not concerned to single out individuals or particular schools or universities for specific criticisms.

Our critique is of the *system*, not of personalities or individual

[1] In the City University Business School, for example, 43 per cent of the MBA
intake over the last two years had an upper second-class (2:1) or higher Honours
degree; 57 per cent had a lower second-class Honours degree or an equivalent
professional qualification; and the ratio of applications to admissions was
100:12. We have no reason to think these figures are untypical of business
schools elsewhere.

institutions. There is much of value in British business schools; but we believe their enormous potential will be unleashed only under a radically different system of property rights. Our intention is not to uproot or destroy what is good in existing schools but to bring about a more favourable climate which will allow their strengths to flourish and develop.

II. THE ORIGINS AND PRESENT STRUCTURE
OF BRITISH BUSINESS SCHOOLS

British business schools were born out of a very particular culture. The economic climate of the early 1960s was interventionist, corporatist and Keynesian. It was the period in which a Conservative Government established the National Economic Development Council (NEDC), and in which a Labour Government secured the agreement of the TUC and employers' organisations to sign the Joint Statement of Intent on Productivity, Prices and Incomes. The Wilson Government, soon after coming into office in 1964, established a Department of Economic Affairs to revitalise the supply side of the economy, a National Plan for economic development, and a National Board for Prices and Incomes to keep continuous watch over price and wage rises. In retrospect, the mid-1960s turned out to be the high-watermark of Keynesian demand management policies and the attempt to launch a Galbraithian new industrial state.

The Robbins Report, 1963

It was against this background that the initial stimulus to the establishment of British business schools was engendered by the Robbins Report of 1963 on the future of higher education in this country. Although the Report was independent, it reflected the views of a number of business leaders as well as corporate bodies such as the NEDC, all of which had been arguing the inadequacies of the existing system of management education and the need for major new developments. The Report was forthright:

'. . . the present educational arrangements for management education are deficient. This country, it is urged, does not provide the training for management that is needed if it is to hold its own in the modern age. Education in individual techniques is provided at the undergraduate level but this is not specifically directed at management. At the postgraduate level, where education of

[23]

this sort should be chiefly at home, there is nothing comparable to the great business schools of the US.'[1]

The Report accepted the diagnosis of the business community and recommended the setting up of two major postgraduate schools. However, two conditions were laid down if the schools were to prosper: first, that they should be linked to well-established institutions of higher education; and, secondly, that they should be situated in the neighbourhood of large business centres. It was recognised explicitly that both conditions were likely to meet one major problem, namely, the salary differentials between academia and business. On the first of these conditions, it was argued that

> 'Problems will arise in such an association: the difficulties about pay differentials in universities may certainly hinder the recruitment of suitable staff' (para. 411).

On location, Robbins was concerned that

> 'The limitation on salary differentials . . . must make it extremely difficult to recruit certain kinds of talent and expert knowledge on a full-time basis' (para. 412).

The Franks Report, 1963

As a result of the public, industrial and academic interest in the idea that business schools on the American model might be set up in the UK, in the summer of 1963 the Federation of British Industries, the BIM, the Federation of Management Education and the NEDC invited Lord Franks to give guidance and advice and to formulate a plan for selecting suitable universities in which the two business schools might be located. He reported within a matter of months.

Franks was convinced of a demand for more and better education and training facilities for business. He recommended the establishment of business schools, 'the primary purpose of which is to be practical, to increase competence in managers or those who will be managers'.[2] His convictions, he said, 'spring from the fact that business management is an intelligent

---

[1] Committee on Higher Education (Chairman: Lord Robbins), *Higher Education: Report*, Cmnd. 2154, HMSO, London, 1963, para. 408.

[2] Lord Franks, *British business schools*, British Institute of Management, London, 1963, para. 3.

form of human activity, not intellectual nor academic, but practical in nature' (para. 6).

But the question which needed to be answered was: Should such a school be part of a university when its *raison d'être* was to be practical, not 'intellectual nor academic'? Robbins had suggested that a school should be part of a university since it would require the strong support of an established institution. Franks did not find that view to be universally shared by industry and commerce. It was held, as might have been expected, by the major educational establishments which would be the principal beneficiaries of the new institutions (para. 12).

Franks gave three reasons for making the schools part of universities. First, US business schools were linked to universities. Secondly, high-calibre staff would not be recruited to business schools from universities if the act of transference meant that they had to sever their university connection. A fundamental tenet of the Franks Report was:

'You cannot just go into the market and buy the staff you want. . . . Adequate background of expert knowledge in all the different disciplines that must be involved can only be provided in this way [as part of a university]' (para. 13).

Thirdly, it was to be expected that graduates seeking a career in business would aim for higher professional qualifications, which it was hoped might take the form of a master's degree.

'But such a degree can only be awarded to someone who is a member of a university and has satisfactorily performed the activities laid down by the university as a qualification' (para. 13).

Like the Robbins Report, however, Franks recognised that the university connection had important implications for salaries:

'. . . from every academic standpoint it is necessary that the salaries paid in the School should be in line with academic salaries generally' (para. 37).

This comparability might result in difficulties in recruiting staff in some areas, but 'nothing substantial [could] be conceded . . . on the general level of salaries' (para. 37). The solution was seen to lie in a general improvement in academic salaries relative to those of business and in outside consulting arrangements for the staff.

[25]

Not surprisingly, the following section of the Report was concerned with the unease felt in *some* academic circles about the intentions of business, and the unease felt in *many* business quarters about the intentions of the universities. The major issue was whether the practical business school desired by Franks could survive in the intellectual, academic, non-practical environment which the universities offered.

The proposition that, because American business schools were linked to universities, British business schools should therefore also be, did not follow automatically. In relation to American business school experience, Franks himself argued that it was impossible to

'transplant it, its way of life, purpose, methods and curricula holus bolus into British soil, and expect the result to be successful. Such attempted transplantation never is . . .' (para. 8).

In addition, Franks paid no heed to the fact that most leading American business schools were part of private universities, whereas in Britain they would be part of the state system.

The claim that the necessary staff could be recruited only within a university system implied a belief that university staff in the new schools would retain the value systems, academic criteria and culture of the departments from which they had transferred. If their reference group was to be their former university peers, what chance had the neglected constituency of industry and commerce? What chance was there of a practical orientation? What hope could there be that the work of the business schools would be 'not intellectual nor academic, but practical in nature'?

Franks's reluctance to enter the market

Franks's remark that 'you cannot just go into the market and buy the staff you want' encapsulated a philosophy more than it stated a truth. That philosophy, which favours public institutions in higher education against private institutions, has rarely been put so succinctly; it expressed a mandarin's distaste for the market-place in education.

The academic reasons for restraining business school salaries within the general salary structure of universities, and for not treating them in a similar manner to medical schools, were not spelled out. And the hope that academic salaries would move upwards to approach salaries in industry and commerce has not been realised; the gap between them has widened so that recruitment of staff of the right quality has become more, not less, difficult.

The proposition that the establishment of a business school would require expert knowledge was never in dispute. But to suggest it could be provided *only* within the confines of a university was too large a claim to sustain without accompanying evidence. That evidence was not provided and the case rested solely on the assertions of the Franks and Robbins Reports.

Although Franks argued that business schools should be established within universities, he nevertheless intended a partnership on the basis of

> 'joint responsibility for the running of the business school; and this must involve joint control of the two basic instruments of management, policy and money. Then and only then will the positive commitment of university and business be sufficient, both being irrevocably involved in the success or failure of the School' (para. 19).

He did not, however, specify in detail the right relationship to give effect to this principle, save to suggest that half the membership of the executive council of the business school should be businessmen, in order to achieve a large measure of autonomy, to prevent any tendency 'to become too theoretical and remote from business', which would be 'disastrous', and to foster a spirit of co-operation with business (paras. 21 and 22).

Franks considered joint partnership not only desirable but a necessity. The potential for friction was, after all, substantial.

> 'Many businessmen, often the men who are most anxious to see Business Schools of the first rank established and functioning . . . fear that the influence of the university will be inimical to the proper purpose of the School. The university, they fear, will make the School over in its own traditional image. Instead of the School being thoroughly vocational and practical, with courses and programmes designed to help managers be better at managing, to increase their general competence, it will become like other departments of a university, concerned with the advancement of knowledge and its communication, turning out scholars and not men better fitted for management. The universities, they believe, are prone to despise applied knowledge and competence . . .' (para. 17).

Franks dismissed business apprehension about how the newly

[27]

established schools might develop with the remark that 'no university is really like this' (para. 17), and buttressed the claims of the universities by asserting that 'the work of a Business School of high quality does not differ from that of any other form of education' (para. 18). The unease of academics focused on the aims, content and duration of courses, as well as on a feeling that they were being asked to be 'magicians not educators' (para. 18). In particular, business favoured shorter, concentrated courses, while academics favoured longer, more general ones. There was, however, general agreement on one issue:

'. . . that the courses for recent graduates should last one year. It was also widely thought that for the foreseeable future it would be unwise to follow the American pattern of two-year courses. A year . . . is enough for the courses to provide valuable training in business studies that have relevance to management later on, and also an education of genuine academic quality' (para. 34).

The implementation of the Franks Report

The Franks Report was implemented by the setting up of the London Business School as an affiliate institution of the University of London, and of the Manchester Business School as a faculty of the University of Manchester. The implementation of the Franks Report, however, differed radically from his original suggestions in five ways:

1. Joint responsiblity for the running of business schools
Instead of the equal partnership proposed in paragraph 20 of the Franks Report, with industry as an equal partner jointly controlling policy and finance ('the two basic instruments of management'), the constitution of the schools resembled, rather, a sole proprietorship. Control was allowed to fall totally into academic hands; business never became an active partner and was relegated to the roles of advisor and fund-raiser.

2. Autonomy within universities
Franks believed that one condition of long-run success was a large measure of autonomy for business schools (para. 21), to be secured by the joint partnership of business and university. The failure of the partnership ideal has inevitably

diminished the autonomy of business schools. Even the London Business School, the most autonomous in the UK, is currently seeking more autonomy from the University of London (with which it has affiliate status) through a Royal Charter.

3. *Recruitment of staff*

Instead of the academic/business mix advocated by Franks, recruitment within the schools has been primarily of academics by academics. A very small proportion of full-time business school staff has had any extended experience of industry and commerce. And the growing disparity of salaries in business schools and industry has made this situation worse. People in industry or commerce are typically able to join business school staffs only on retirement, with their pensions making up the difference.

4. *Value system*

From their inception, UK business schools recruited staff primarily from related university disciplines. This, together with their location within a university structure, has meant that staff have carried over the same expectations, value systems and career ambitions into what they generally thought of as just another, if newer, university department. The market need for vocational orientation was paid lip-service only since the internal criteria for promotion remained primarily, if not exclusively, academic.

5. *Course content and direction*

Both the content and direction of courses were determined by academic institutions, not by business. Even the specific advice of the Franks Report that the courses should last only one year has been totally disregarded by the two designated business schools—London Business School and Manchester Business School.

It is perhaps not too much to say that, once in the driving seat, the universities adopted what was congenial to them in Franks and discarded the rest. But it is difficult to see what else could have happened since Franks specifically eschewed the market mechanism as a means of control and suggested no alternative regulatory body or system to make business schools adhere to the aims and purposes of his Report.

TABLE I

POSTGRADUATE BUSINESS EDUCATION IN BRITAIN: COURSES, STAFF AND STUDENTS, 1982-83

Institution	Postgraduate degree or diploma	Total full-time equivalent student loads			Full-time academic staff	
		Undergraduate	Postgraduate Research	Postgraduate Taught	Wholly university financed	Other
Aston	Diploma/MBA	627	27	250	67	8
Bath	MSc Bus. Admin.	257	94	36	36	4
Bradford	MBA	332	31	149	43	35
Brunel	MBA	38	48	89	4	–
City	MBA	205	22	234	33	12
Durham	MSc Man. Studs.	23	1	39	12	5
Hull		84	1	1	7	–
Kent		50	3	11	4	–
Lancaster	MA	274	36	171	38	2
Leeds	MBA	183	2	20	12	–
London Business School	MSc Bus. Admin.	–	41	198	33	27
London University	MSc Man. Studs.	147	55	209	28	6
Loughborough	MSc Man. Studs.	406	12	26	33	2
Manchester Business School	Diploma/MBA	–	29	229	36	9
UMIST	Diploma/MSc Man. Science	667	106	61	50	7
Oxford		18	10	24	3	–
Salford		258	5	24	26	–
Sheffield	Diploma/Bus. Studies	436	9	21	34	–
Warwick	MBA	193	24	86	29	7
Total England		**4,198**	**551**	**1,878**	**528**	**124**

TABLE I [continued]

POSTGRADUATE BUSINESS EDUCATION IN BRITAIN: COURSES, STAFF AND STUDENTS, 1982-83

Institution	Postgraduate degree or diploma	Total full-time equivalent student loads			Full-time academic staff	
		Undergraduate	Postgraduate		Wholly university financed	Other
			Research	Taught		
Cardiff University College		86	9	10	10	–
UWIST	Diploma/MSc	160	12	32	14	–
Total Wales		**246**	**21**	**42**	**24**	**–**
Edinburgh	Diploma/MBA	313	10	50	20	1
Glasgow	MBA	29	9	69	11	8
Heriot-Watt	MSc Man. Studs.	223	3	50	19	–
Stirling		137	8	6	12	2
Strathclyde	MBA	502	26	250	58	17
Total Scotland		**1,204**	**56**	**425**	**120**	**28**
Total Great Britain		**5,648**	**628**	**2,345**	**672**	**152**
Queen's University Belfast	Diploma/MBA	142	7	43	12	–
Total N. Ireland		**142**	**7**	**43**	**12**	**–**
Total UK		**5,790**	**635**	**2,388**	**684**	**152**

Source: Universities' Statistical Record, *University Statistics 1982-3, Vol. 6, Finance,* Table 9 (xiv).

[31]

Business education in Britain is by no means the monopoly of business schools; it takes place through a variety of institutions, such as polytechnics, technical colleges, independent management colleges and, to no small extent, the in-house training facilities of companies themselves. Nevertheless, business schools form an important part of the whole scene.

Since the establishment of the London and Manchester Business Schools in 1965, numerous other business schools and departments of management have come into existence in British universities. Table I lists those universities which currently offer MBA or MBA-equivalent courses. The list includes Henley, which was established in 1946 as the Administrative Staff College and is now linked to Brunel University. But it does not include the Cranfield School of Management, which is part of the Cranfield Institute of Technology and which differs from other universities in that it is funded directly by the Department of Education and Science and *not* through the University Grants Committee.

Size and product mix

Existing British business schools produce a number of quite separate products: full-time and part-time MBA programmes, undergraduate degrees in business, research degrees in business, short-term post-experience courses, programmes tailored exclusively for individual companies, and research.

As can be seen from Table I, business schools vary enormously in size, judged by either numbers of students or staffing. Some, such as Aston, Bradford and Strathclyde, are very large in terms of students, while others are rather small, such as Brunel, Cardiff, Durham and Oxford. Some have a major preponderance of undergraduates on taught courses (Bath, Leeds), while others are exclusively postgraduate (London and Manchester Business Schools), and yet others have a substantial number of each (Aston, City and Strathclyde). Since the recent cuts in public spending on higher education, several schools have established part-time degrees (Table II). Some, such as London Business School, Manchester Business School and the City University Business School, run many post-experience and company programmes, while others do little in this area.

TABLE II

PART-TIME MBAs IN UK BUSINESS SCHOOLS AND UNIVERSITIES: SOME COURSE INFORMATION, 1983*

Institution and Degree	Offered since	Students admitted in current year	Relation to full-time MBA	Staff paid for MBA teaching?
Aston: MBA	1976	53	Fully integrated	No
Bradford: MBA	1982	43	Distinct	No
City: MBA	1983	89	Moving to full integration	Yes
Cranfield: MBA	1981	35	Distinct	No
Durham: MBA	n.a.	n.a.	n.a.	n.a.
Edinbrugh: MBA	1984	n.a.	n.a.	Yes
Glasgow: MBA	1976	43	No full-time	No
London Business School: MSc	1983	60	Equivalent	No
Loughborough: MSc	1982	30	No full-time	No
Manchester Business School: MBSc	1981	15	Some joint activities	No
Newcastle: MBA	1980	22	No full-time	No
Strathclyde: MBA	1976	62	Closely related	Yes
UMIST: MSc	1982	45	Closely related	No
University of Ulster: MBA	1980	18	No full-time	No
Warwick: MBA	1981	3	Closely related	No

* Some schools now offering both full and part-time options have not been included in this list.

Source: The Business Graduate, January 1984.

[33]

British business schools also vary widely in their organisational attachment to universities. The London Business School, for example, was established as an independent corporate entity limited by guarantee, having affiliate status with the University of London but negotiating its grant of public money directly with the UGC. The School is governed by a Council but final academic authority is vested in the University. The Manchester Business School is a faculty of Manchester University, but with a high degree of automony. It negotiates directly with the UGC for its funding and is governed by its Council, which reports to the University Council annually—with, once again, the Senate of the University having final authority over academic matters. Most other business schools (Aston, Bradford, City, Strathclyde) are either schools or departments of the universities of which they are part and are therefore answerable to the senate and council of their universities. The allocation of public funds to such schools is decided by university committees, and not as with London and Manchester, by direct negotiation with the UGC.

As can be seen from Table I, 80 per cent of full-time academic staff at British business schools are financed by public funds. This aggregate figure, however, conceals wide differences: for Manchester Business School the figure is 80 per cent; for London Business School it is only 55 per cent, while for some, such as Salford and Sheffield, it is 100 per cent.

Although British business schools show considerable diversity, it must nevertheless be emphasised in conclusion that, with the exception of Cranfield:

(a) all British business schools are attached to British universities;

(b) all schools abide by the UGC cartel in the minimum fees they charge students;

(c) the salaries of business school staff are fixed on the agreed UGC scale and life tenure is the standard expectation of most staff;

(d) the ethos of all schools is indistinguishable from that of a university; and

(e) no British business school has less than 50 per cent public funding.

[34]

III. EXPLAINING THE LACK OF SUCCESS

Three major hypotheses

A variety of explanations are typically advanced to account for the relative lack of success of British business schools. They include such factors as 'the peculiar social and cultural values' of Britain, the 'traditions, suspicions, prejudices and power of the universities', 'MBAs are an expensive luxury', 'MBAs don't fit in', the irrelevance of business schools to practical business, and the bad experience of companies in hiring MBAs. Three major explanations of the relative lack of success of British business schools emerge from an examination of these criticisms.

(i) *The corporate culture of British business*

This explanation places responsibility firmly with the business community, in terms of factors influencing the corporate *demand* for MBAs. *Either* the attitudes of British companies are such that, regardless of commercial considerations, they do not (with some notable exceptions) wish to hire MBAs; *or*, given the quality of the products of the business schools, the price being asked by MBAs is too high.

It is important to separate these two major factors. It is perfectly reasonable for a company not to hire MBAs if their value to it is less than the expected salary. But this is a very different kind of argument from that which contends that the culture of British business, unlike that of American companies, is not only anti-intellectual but unable to see a commercial proposition when it is made. The argument about corporate culture seems to us to run contrary to the fact that, over the past 20 years, British business has made increasing use of post-experience facilities at recognised business schools and management colleges (such as Ashridge and Sundridge Park), has sponsored undergraduate business courses in a number of universities and polytechnics, and has established a growing number of in-house graduate training programmes. Such evidence suggests that the corporate culture of British companies is not opposed to graduate training in business, but that companies much prefer in-house training programmes and post-experience courses, over which they can exercise control, to the formal MBA programmes designed almost exclusively by academics.

(ii) *Academic culture of British business schools*

The explanation frequently put forward by business is that what business schools teach is far too academic, and that some of it is irrelevant for practical business purposes. It is difficult to deny that business schools are more academic than practical institutions. The interesting question, however, is *why* this is so and why it should continute to remain so if the MBAs they produce do not satisfy the market demand.

(iii) *A cartel funded and directed by government*

A third explanation blames the relative failure of business schools on an inefficient market in formal business education, itself the consequence of government subsidies to the producing firms, cartelised pricing agreements within the industry, a government-imposed salary structure, and the imposition of quotas on the outputs of each institution.

Industrial organisation of British universities

Since all British business schools (with the exception of Cranfield School of Management) are linked to British universities, it is necessary to examine the industrial organisation of British universities if we are to understand the nature of the problem with the schools. Traditionally, British universities have been considered autonomous institutions which expect and enjoy a large measure of freedom over their use of funds. At the same time, university education is supplied by an industry which is funded primarily by government (with the exception of the University of Buckingham), whose total output is fixed by government, in which individual 'firms' are subject to detailed production quotas, in which prices and wages are determined along the lines of a classic cartel, and whose employees are typically granted security of tenure for life.

Government funding

Direct government funding of British universities accounts for approximately 80 per cent of their income (Table III). The funds for the recurrent grant are voted by Parliament and form part of the departmental budget of the Department of Education & Science (DES). They are then allocated to individual universities and certain institutions by the University Grants Committee (UGC),[1] which was set up in 1919 to stand between government and the universities to protect their freedom.

For home students, universities also receive fees which are paid by local government at the undergraduate level and by central government at the postgraduate level. In 1982-83, the most recent year for which information is available, fees charged to students accounted for only about 10 per cent of total public sector funding of the universities, while the UGC recurrent grant accounted for 80 per cent. In the same year, public funding constituted roughly 80 per cent of university funding while other income constituted only 17 per cent of total funding. This contrasts with the early days of the UGC when the then government grant amounted to only 30 per cent of university income.[2]

Even though the revenue of business schools is made up of non-UGC finance to a much larger extent than most other university departments, the fact that they are part of publicly-funded institutions is crucial. Our thesis is that institutions which are 80 per cent publicly funded develop an ethos which is risk-averse, secure and non-entrepreneurial, and that this becomes a dominant influence on business schools which are a part of universities.

[1] The amended terms of reference of the UGC in 1946 were:

'To inquire into the financial needs of university education in Great Britain; to advise the government as to the application of any grants made by Parliament towards meeting them; to collect, examine and make available information relating to university education throughout the United Kingdom, and to assist, in consultation with the universities and other bodies concerned, the preparation and execution of such plans for the development of the universities as may from time to time be required in order to ensure that they are fully adequate to national needs.'

(Committee on Higher Education, *Higher Education*, Appendix Four: *Administrative, Financial and Economic Aspects of Higher Education*, Cmnd. 2154-IV, HMSO, 1963.)

[2] *A Strategy for Higher Education into the 1990s: The University Grants Committee's Advice*, HMSO, September 1984, p. 34.

[37]

TABLE III

PUBLIC AND OTHER FUNDING OF BRITISH
UNIVERSITIES, 1982-83

Public Funding	£ million	%
UGC recurrent grant	1,205	
Home student fees and research training support grants	150	
Research grants from Research Councils	114	
Computer Board grants	16	
	1,485	79
Other Income		
Endowments, donations and subscriptions	20	
Services rendered:	307	
Overseas students' fees (83)		
Research grants (other than from Research Councils) and contracts (145)		
Other items, including continuing education (79)		
Other sources	66	
	393	21
TOTAL	1,878	100

Source: A Strategy for Higher Education into the 1990s: The University Grants Committee's Advice, HMSO, September 1984, p. 34.

Department of Education and Science production quotas

Traditionally, the DES has given a block grant to each university through the UGC, without directives as to how it should be disbursed (which is in marked contrast to the funding of colleges and polytechnics). During the period since the Robbins Report of 1963, however, the autonomy of universities has been much less than might have been imagined from the formal description of this arrangement. Detailed standards have been laid down for capital expenditure on buildings, furniture and equipment, for example. In the post-

Robbins period, the UGC itself has described its role as adopting an 'increasingly active interpretation' of its guidelines.[1]

Recently, this process has been taken a stage further. In implementing the public expenditure cuts of 1980 to 1983, the DES has placed what amounts to production quotas on all universities (in the form of maximum numbers for home students in arts and science). For example, the principles underlying the UGC's budget cuts of 1981 and 1982 were that reductions should be applied selectively, and that appropriate guidance should be given to universities to help in the restructuring of provision, with a change in the distribution of students towards natural science and technology.[2]

The 'guidance' given to universities was of a very precise and detailed nature. Since then, by announcing extra resources for 'new-blood' posts and for posts in information technology, the UGC (together with the Research Councils) has become even more involved in the detailed allocation of resources to and by individual institutions. These controls are imposed on mainstream academic courses, and not on the other business school products such as short courses, in-house training, and 'distance learning' (by video, for example), which are seen as peripheral activities by the business schools. They are necessary, not for the development of subjects or academic staff, but simply for the funding of mainstream activities which might otherwise be curtailed.

Cartelised pricing and behaviour

Another feature of British universities is that price competition (fees for courses) between individual 'firms' (universities) is strictly limited. Universities adhere to a set of minimum prices fixed by government, as shown, for example, by the minimum fixed-price structure for student fees for the current academic year in Table IV.

The letter from the Chairman of the UGC to individual universities in which the pricing structure is set out emphasises that the fees are minimum and not average, thereby restricting any possible competition which might emerge on that score. In addition, the notes accompanying the figures are careful to

[1] UGC, *University Development 1962-67*, Cmnd. 3820, HMSO, 1968.

[2] Letter from the Secretary of State for Education and Science to the Chairman of the UGC (14 July 1982), in *University Grants Committee Annual Survey: Academic Year 1982-83*, Appendix C, Cmnd. 8965, HMSO, July 1983.

[39]

TABLE IV

CARTELISED PRICING STRUCTURE OF BRITISH UNIVERSITIES, 1984-85

Type of postgraduate course	Student fees (per year)	
	Home £	Overseas £
Arts courses	1,569	3,150
Science courses	1,569	4,150
Clinical courses in medicine, dentistry and veterinary science	1,569	7,650

Source: University Grants Committee, Information Department.

include precise definitions of what constitutes science and arts courses—presumably to prevent individual institutions from attempting to draw up definitions to their own competitive advantage.[1]

From the published material of the UGC, therefore, it is evident that British universities operate a classic price cartel: they fix prices among themselves for the services they produce rather than allow them to be market-determined, thereby restricting competition. And as with other cartels, the universities' one is swift to respond to changes in the market-place. For example, in 1979 the Government decided that it should no longer subsidise overseas students and that universities should charge 'full cost'. Recognising the resulting scope for competitive pricing, the UGC quickly stepped in:

[1] '*Note 1*: [Arts] courses are intended to be those which do not involve significant laboratory or workshop or studio-based activities. Arts courses which do involve such facilities should, at the discretion of the universities, be charged as 'Science courses'; whereas mathematics (where distinguishable from computer sciences) might be classified as 'arts'.

'*Note 2*: Science courses for this purpose may be taken to mean laboratory, etc., based courses, and at the discretion of the universities might include courses in the arts, social sciences and pre-clinical medicine, dentistry and veterinary studies where the costs involved are likely to be on a similar scale.

'*Note 3*: This recommendation [for fees for clinical courses] is intended to relate to the clinical stages of medicine and dentistry, where these are clearly distinguishable, and for the later practical stages of veterinary studies. Where these stages are not clear-cut, universities should adapt the recommendations so that their costs are covered.'

(Letter from Edward Parkes, Chairman of the UGC, to Vice-Chancellors and Principals, dated 23 January 1981.)

[40]

'Since the change in Government policy . . . the Committee has, after consultation with the Committee of Vice-Chancellors and Principals, recommended to universities minimum fees for over-seas students. We are likely to continue to do this for another year or so in order to smooth the transition to a more competitive régime.'[1]

So far there has been no recognition that the transition is over!

The survival of a cartel and the degree of collusion which its members can maintain depend crucially on the extent to which entry into the industry can be successfully blocked. The major conclusion established by empirical studies of pricing behaviour is that cartels typically erect barriers to entry and, whenever possible, obtain government support for both entry barriers and the policing of the cartel agreements. Unlike OPEC, the building societies, opticians, solicitors or the Stock Exchange, universities have succeeded in achieving both. The universities' cartel has now survived for almost 40 years.

A major entry barrier which dissuades new private insti-tutions from establishing themselves as universities in Britain is that the power to confer degrees must first be granted by royal charter or by statute. Private business colleges (such as Ashridge and Sundridge Park) suffer a major handicap by comparison with business schools, precisely because they lack the ability to confer degrees. Another entry barrier is the large government subsidy to existing 'firms'. Even among those business schools which derive a substantial proportion of their income from non-UGC sources, such as London, Manchester and Cranfield, the size of the continuing state subsidy is still sufficiently large to act as a significant deterrent to new entrants.

The role of government in supporting the universities' cartel is implemented through a complex and informal set of relation-ships between the UGC and the Committee of Vice-Chancellors and Principals (CVCP) by which the UGC not only protects British universities from new entrants but also polices the existing cartel agreements.

Again, because of the restrictions on price competition, most cartels experience a chiselling of prices at the margin by members seeking to gain an edge. The same holds true for universities, and especially in management and business. Post-experience courses are designed so that they are excluded from

[1] University Grants Committee, *A Strategy* . . ., *op. cit.*, para. 9.13.

the cartel structure and universities vie with each other to gain sponsorships to enable them to reduce prices.

A further feature of cartel behaviour is that the restriction of price competition diverts competition for market share between member firms into quality and design. Thus the clearing banks' cartel before 1971, like the building societies' cartel today, resulted in excessive competition to establish new branches and design new products. In the case of the Stock Exchange, the cartel has produced excessive research output. Competition in quality and design is precisely what is observed in the academic world: individual universities vying with one another in academic standards, innovation in new courses and teaching methods, and the introduction of new subjects and facilities for students.

Non-price competition is not objectionable in itself. The objection is simply that when used as a substitute for price competition it results in an inefficient allocation of resources for society as a whole.

Fixed salary scales

Typically, members of a cartel are interested not only in restricting competition among themselves in the price of their product or service but also in limiting competition on the cost side. From its origin in 1919, the UGC monitored university salaries but was strongly of the opinion that they should not be standardised. In 1930, for example, it stated:

> '. . . we have expressed [ourselves] on previous occasions adverse to any general scheme applicable to all university institutions and providing for uniform fixed salary scales in automatic increments. Each university or college must be free to decide for itself what is best suited to its own needs and resources, and it is not only natural but desirable that the size, wealth and standing of different institutions should be reflected by differences in salaries'.[1]

In 1946 under the Attlee Government, the UGC, quite contrary to its earlier policy, laid down a standard rate for professorial salaries after consultation with the Treasury. This time it opined:

> 'There can, in the judgement of the Committee, be no justification for the utilisation of a largely increased Exchequer grant for the

---

[1] Quoted in National Board for Prices and Incomes, *Standing Reference on the Pay of University Teachers*, Report 98, Cmnd. 3866, HMSO, December 1968.

purpose of raising salaries beyond the level which the Treasury are prepared to subsidise'.[1]

In 1948 the Spens Committee laid down a standardised scale for medical consultants and specialists working in universities. And in 1949 a new national salary structure, which covered all academic staff, was introduced, together with a ceiling on the ratio of senior to junior staff. Only Oxford and Cambridge and clinical staff of medical schools refused to be part of this system.

More recently, the Committee of Vice-Chancellors and Principals have been quite explicit about the purpose of their national structure:

> 'When the concept of a maximum permitted ratio of senior academic staff was introduced in 1949 the purpose was to ensure that broadly similar career prospects were available in all universities and so minimise competition between universities for scarce staff'.[2]

It is remarkable that the Association of University Teachers (AUT), which is ostensibly concerned with increasing the real income of its members, is a partner to this arrangement.

Security of tenure

A fifth feature of higher education is security of tenure whereby a member of the academic staff of a university is typically offered a contract guaranteeing job security until retirement, other than for 'good cause'. In a recent survey of opinion in universities, the UGC found that

> 'Tenure provisions . . . are strongly defended by most universities as a way of protecting academic freedom and the long-term investment by individuals and institutions in their teaching, research and scholarship'.[3]

Yet in the opinion of the recent Jarratt Report on efficiency in

---

[1] Quoted in University Grants Committee, *Report on University Development 1957-62*, Cmnd. 2267, HMSO, February 1964, p. 138.

[2] Committee of Vice-Chancellors and Principals of the Universities of the United Kingdom, *Annual Report 1983-84*, para. 5.3.

[3] University Grants Committee, *A Strategy . . .*, *op. cit.*, p. 66, Annex C, Digest of Replies to Circular Letter 16/83, Question 23. Respondents included 55 institutions on the UGC grant list and the Northern Ireland universities, 11 vice-chancellors and principals on the grant list, 115 national organisations, inter-university and non-university bodies, 370 groups within universities, and 107 individuals.

the universities, tenure 'has inhibited change and even the discussion of change' in British universities.[1]

Consequences of public funding and the cartel

Public funding and the cartelised nature of the universities have had profound effects on the ethos, conduct, structure and performance of British business schools.

First, public money has driven a wedge between the consumer (business) and the producer (business schools), and thus introduced an inefficiency into the market for business education. Inefficiency is used here in the strictly economic sense that, because property rights within the market are so ill-defined, producers fail to respond to the wants of consumers. As Adam Smith observed over 200 years ago:

> 'The discipline of colleges and universities is in general contrived, not for the benefit of students, but for the interest, or more properly speaking, the ease of the masters. Its object is, in all cases, to maintain the authority of the master, and whether he neglects or performs his duty, to oblige the students in all cases to behave to him as if he performed it with the greatest diligence and ability'.[2]

This is an inefficiency currently evidenced in British business schools in a number of ways: complaints by students about the uneven quality of teaching; the design of the curriculum by academic staff with little business involvement; the research efforts of staff being oriented towards traditional academic journals rather than towards the solution of business problems; and the patchy quality of the administrative services provided by the schools to their students.

Second, risk-taking is being taught in and by a risk-averse culture. The cartelised nature of higher education and the job security which university appointments have traditionally offered have tended to create an ethos within universities which is conducive to leisurely and scholarly reflection rather than risk-taking. While this ethos may be entirely appropriate for certain subjects and for fundamental research, it is hardly

---

[1] Committee of Vice-Chancellors and Principals, *Report of the Steering Committee for Efficiency Studies in Universities* (The Jarratt Report), March 1985, p. 10, Section 2.7d.

[2] Adam Smith, *An Inquiry into the Nature and Causes of the Wealth of Nations* (1776), 1976 edition, p. 764, para. 16.

appropriate for those who teach business. Whilst the latter shelter in a protected and secure part of the public sector, those who practise business are exposed to a highly uncertain and changing environment. The major effect is that the interests of staff, their research focus, and the changing emphasis of the curriculum will all tend to reflect the internal rather than the external environment.

Third, public funding and the accompanying rigidities lead to dynamic inefficiency—the failure of institutions to respond to shifts in consumer demand. This case has been cogently argued by Professor Peter Moore, Principal of the London Business School and a former Chairman of the Management Sub-Committee of the UGC:

> 'While new areas of study can be readily developed in times of institutional expansion, it has proved difficult with level funding or retrenchment to make changes in the balance of subjects or of the position of courses within the system. If student and employer demand, with their relatively frequent shifts of emphasis, become prime determinants, this inflexibility could prove a stumbling block. Unlike comparable institutions in many parts of the world, the staff proportion in the UK on permanent contract is high'.[1]

The dilemma is that, while flexibility is required to meet changes in demand, any shift in subject balance is impeded, if not blocked, by the rigidities imposed by the present system. Given static funding or retrenchment, university departments are constrained within a zero-sum game in which gains in some subjects must be at the expense of losses in others. Those subjects with declining demand or students of below-average quality have a considerable vested interest in restricting change to a minimum, and do so. On the other hand, subjects with a high growth potential and above-average student quality are stifled by inadequate support, insufficient funding and under-staffing. To continue the zero-sum game, however, will lead to increased friction and in-fighting between the business schools and other university departments. Business schools see themselves as continually under-funded, frustrated, and liable to fail in realising their potential, because the universities do not have the resources to match the business schools' growth possibilities. At the same time, any department living on the

---

[1] Peter G. Moore, 'Higher education: the next decade', *Journal of the Royal Statistical Society*, Vol. 146, Part 3, 1983.

margin will view even the small reductions in their allocations, which are made to placate the business schools, as too much for them to be able to bear and survive. They see business schools as unduly pampered and ungrateful for the sacrifices that other departments have made. The business schools in turn see themselves as being starved of the funds necessary to achieve their objectives and realise their potential.

Fourth, there is the intellectual dominance of business schools by the traditional disciplines of social science. The social sciences are essentially concerned with the *observation* of business: the collection of data on performance, the development and testing of hypotheses, and the establishment of general principles. In economics, it is about how markets work, how relative prices are determined, and how resources are allocated. In psychology, it is about learning, motivation, attitudes and perception. In finance, it is about the determination of asset prices.

The social scientist is an individual viewing the game from the grandstand. But management is not concerned with the observation of business: it is about playing the game itself. While the results of social science provide useful background and insights for management education, managers themselves are more concerned with the skills, tactics and strategy of how to play the game and improve their play. Arguably, this is the most under-developed and under-researched aspect of management education. British business schools have a preponderance of staff who are trained in the techniques of social science and whose outlook is therefore frequently constrained by their experience. At the same time, the schools have a lack of staff with experience of playing the game. This is not to say that the academic disciplines of social science have *no* place in a business school curriculum. They most certainly do. But they should form a background to the real issues of business rather than constitute the major part of the training, as at present.

Fifth, business schools which are linked to universities are inexorably a part of university decision-making machinery. This aspect has recently been evaluated by the UGC itself. Its conclusions are devastating.

'In the universities tradition and inertia often work against change. In particular, in the Senate the practitioners of existing subjects are present to make their case, while the practitioners of the potential new subjects are not. Universities need to acquire what they now lack: a deliberate bias towards change.

'This criticism is not the only one that can be made of the machinery of government of universities. Much of the activity of academics consists of re-examining received notions; and it is an axiom that, however decisive an argument may appear to be, one must not rule out the possibility that new and unforeseeable considerations may undermine it. In research, which is a perfectionist activity, this is essential. Everyday administration should not be like that, but typically decisions in a university are put forward by a subordinate committee and then reconsidered by a hierarchy of further committees piled on top of it. This may improve the quality of the decisions, but at the price of a great deal of delay and a great diversion of time and energy of academics from their prime functions of teaching and research. In our judgement, the cost often outweighs the gain.

'The position has become more serious in the last few years, because contraction is inevitably more controversial than expansion. We have been struck by the number of complaints we have heard from academics that they have been distracted from teaching and research by the increasing number of committees on which they have to serve.'[1]

Sixth, because business schools are more exposed to the forces of the market than some other parts of universities, they are compelled to develop practices and set up institutions which circumvent the cartel. If business schools are to hire first-class staff with a business orientation and experience, they must be prepared to pay salaries which are market-related. Franks acknowledged this problem and thought it could be solved by using the full range of professorial salaries, consultancy fees and directorships. In practice, it cannot and has not. When a national salary scale for university staff was introduced in 1949, it created the concept of a rate of pay for a university lecturer regardless of discipline. It is quite appropriate that business school staff should be paid at the same rate as pure mathematicians, theoretical physicists, Greek specialists and molecular biologists, *first*, if they are viewed and view themselves primarily as university teachers, and, *second*, if the relative scales of pay in outside employment are roughly equal for each subject category of university staff. In our judgement, neither of these holds.

[1] University Grants Committee, *A Strategy* . . ., *op. cit.*, para. 10.11 and 10.12.

To compound the problems, the nationally negotiated university scale for lecturers is one of the largest in the public sector. It has been described by one researcher, Dr Peter Knight, as

'. . . unimaginative, plodding and designed to discourage creativity and eliminate incentives. It is a scale for time-servers. It is inescapable that, once appointed to the scale, individuals will creep up to the maximum with only minor variations in the speed at which they achieve that goal. The only opportunities for rewarding merit remain in promotion to a more senior post. It is surprising that in a community that is meant to encourage initiative and reward creativity the basic salary scale should be such as to discourage such activities and to provide the minimum possible opportunity for rewarding them.'[1]

If that applies to universities as a whole, it surely applies *a fortiori* to business schools.

The results of attempting to insulate business school salaries from those of the market are that: (*a*) business schools find it extremely difficult to hire first-class businessmen who have a talent for teaching and research, and (*b*) business schools have to set up various schemes to create flexibility in the salary structure which invariably are contrary to the whole financial ethos of the universities of which they are part. While the latter certainly enable business schools to hire first-class staff and develop post-experience courses, they are an inadequate substitute for market-related salaries in that they distract from the central task of developing the substance of business education.

A note of caution

At the end of Section II we stated quite explicitly that British business schools are far from homogeneous. They differ in size, constitution, funding and product mix. Despite these differences, however, we found that there are certain common characteristics. It is because all schools are substantially publicly funded, members of the UGC cartel, and subject to UGC constraints on the use of public money that the analysis of this section is relevant to *all* schools. They are all fundamentally

[1] Peter Knight, 'Terms of Employment', in A. Morris and J. Sizer (eds.), *Resources and Higher Education*, Leverhulme Programme of Study into the Future of Higher Education, 1982, p. 1,906.

producer-driven and are all part of a system which could be considerably improved to serve the nation better.

Having said this, however, a note of caution is required. Because they are not all funded by government to the same degree, and because the nature of their constitutions allows some more freedom than others, the criticisms we have advanced do not apply to all schools equally.

IV. A PLAN FOR REFORM

The case for radical change

The very fact that there is such widespread scepticism in British business about the contribution of British business schools is a sufficiently powerful reason for reforming the present system. But it might still be asked: Why do we need such a radical change? Could not business schools be reformed within the present system? Certainly marginal improvements can be made and, indeed, are being made. But we are convinced that such changes will remain marginal and be nowhere near as effective as those required for the system to meet the real needs of business.

In the first place, a fundamental change is required in the whole ethos of business school education, which is not possible as long as the strong links with universities continue. Since the major criticism made by business is that business schools are too academic, their ethos must be changed so that:

(a) their primary aim would be to increase the effectiveness of managers and those who will be managers;

(b) the primary function of all staff members would be to direct teaching, research and publication to achieve that aim;

(c) the reference group for business school staff would be not fellow academics in the same discipline in other universities but managers in business;

(d) the selection, evaluation and promotion criteria for staff would be based on their relative success in furthering the primary aim in each function.

We believe that the nature of the relationship between universities and business schools was not fully confronted by Robbins and Franks. Both implicitly accepted (*a*) and (*b*) as desirable characteristics of business schools, but wished to graft the new institutions onto existing university structures. They therefore, by implication, rejected (*c*) and (*d*). If there is to be a new ethos, *a joint partnership between industry and business school staff will be required*, of the kind envisaged but not realised by the Franks Report, with joint responsibility for policy and monetary controls, curriculum content and relevance, curriculum and course development, recruitment of students and staff, and student placement, so that the key partnership will be with the external market-place of the business world and not the internal one with other traditional academic departments of the same university.

For this new ethos to be realised, the kind of business school we envisage will be totally unlike any other part of the university. Its primary aim will be to develop the skills, insights and theory relevant to business. It will require its staff to teach, research and publish to achieve this practical objective. Selection, evaluation and promotion will be decided on the basis of criteria different from other university departments. In those departments, the key to promotion is strictly academic achievement within a particular discipline, resulting in publication in a referred journal of repute in that discipline. Relevance, practicality and application to real-world decision-making are achieved by accident, if at all. This is not to decry such research or publication, but to recognise that its purpose is to develop a particular discipline, often to higher levels of abstraction.

These distinctions are especially important because the universities see one of their roles *vis-à-vis* the business schools as to guarantee academic standards. The maintenance of academic standards is sought by means of course committees, academic policy committees, and university senates, which consist of academics recruited from other departments. Such a system of like judging like has value when there is a common aim, identical requirements of staff, similar academic reference groups, and comparable criteria of selection, evaluation and promotion. But what happens when the business school differs from other university departments in all these features? The pressure of the rest of the university on the business school, albeit unconscious, is to make it conform. That is what they have done in the past and will continue to do in the future. It is this conflict which is at the root of the problem.

Separation is, however, necessary on other grounds also. A school which is, as Franks suggested, operationally and financially a joint venture of university staff and outside business and commercial personnel does not easily fit into a university structure. That is why the universities ensured that such a school did not come into being after the Franks Report. And the universities have a case since they are not constituted to handle an institution such as a business school with fundamental differences in aims, staff function, reference groups, selection evaluation and promotion criteria, composition and organisation. But instead of recognising the differences and the need for complete separation, the universities' solution was (and remains) to emasculate the business schools, incorporating them within university structures so that they have the full confidence of neither the business community nor the academic community at large.

Finally, radical change is required because the freedom of action of business schools and universities within the present publicly-funded cartel is exceedingly limited. The key changes which are necessary if truly entrepreneurial institutions are to be created, namely a competitive fee structure and competitive salaries, run totally counter to the existing cartel agreements. Any significant attempts at even piecemeal change would undermine the system itself and would, therefore, in all probability be resisted.

A six-point plan for reform

(1) Undergraduate business education to be separated from postgraduate business education

Since this *Hobart Paper* aims at the reform of postgraduate business education, a division between postgraduate and undergraduate business education is necessary. This is not because we are averse to the radical reform of undergraduate education, but simply because it would raise many issues which distract from and complicate the present analysis.

(2) All postgraduate business schools to become autonomous legal entities independent of the public sector

If business schools are to respond quickly to changing market demands and become more integrated with business, it is important that they become legal entities in their own right, completely independent of the public sector.

One possible model for postgraduate business schools would

be to seek charity status and become companies limited by guarantee on the lines of the London Business School. The new constitution would define the nature of the schools' activities and remove the present fallback position whereby the taxpayer, via the university, the UGC and government, makes good any losses. Other possible models would be private companies, or partnerships of staff, or combinations of the two.

(3) *All postgraduate business school activity to cease being government funded over a three-year period*

(a) It is proposed that all public funding of current expenditure be phased out over three years, after which all graduate business schools would be expected to earn sufficient current income by selling their services in the market-place to ensure survival and growth.

(b) It is proposed that annual capital funding should also terminate at the end of the third year; however, because of the necessity for an endowment to cover capital costs, it is suggested that a seven-year capital funding level be given 'en bloc' at the end of the third year. Private capital funding would then be sought to complement this.

(c) It is proposed that all Economic and Social Research Council (ESRC) studentships for MBA-equivalent courses be withdrawn after three years.

(4) *Salaries and terms and conditions of employment at the private postgraduate business schools to be market-determined*

Since the schools will be 'islanded' and their success made dependent upon the market, staff salaries and terms and conditions of employment would become market determined. A free market in staff employment would permit a large variety of possible contracts to be introduced, ranging from short-term fixed contracts to open contracts. Some might even include tenure, but tenure would be guaranteed not by the taxpayer but by the continuing success of the organisation. Staff wishing to retain current terms and conditions of employment would have to transfer to undergraduate courses at the university with which the business school was associated. There is nothing

TABLE V

ACADEMIC DEPARTMENTAL EXPENDITURE: BRITISH BUSINESS SCHOOLS, 1982/83

Departmental recurrent expenditure (£000s)

Institution	From general income				Specific expenditure		Departmental equipment expenditure
	Total	Salaries of academic and related staff	Other salaries and wages	Other expenditure	Research grants and contracts	Other	
Aston	1,390	1,084	212	94	99	–	69
Bath	708	620	53	35	89	49	23
Bradford	843	720	84	39	130	948	23
Brunel	334	–	–	334	–	–	–
City	901	575	137	190	180	492	20
Durham	186	140	22	24	116	240	–
Hull	135	119	5	11	–	–	–
Kent	73	68	4	1	–	–	–
Lancaster	989	835	71	84	38	5	2
Leeds	262	219	28	15	-33	25	3
London Business School	810	499	92	219	640	554	60
London University	909	769	112	27	172	18	47
Loughborough	662	578	44	40	42	48	8
Manchester Business School	858	683	167	8	196	857	30
UMIST	1,073	885	99	88	100	29	92
Oxford	236	47	–	189	–	–	–
Salford	515	451	52	13	3	–	9
Sheffield	607	554	45	8	1	1	13
Warwick	645	577	36	32	129	73	5
Total England	**12,138**	**9,423**	**1,263**	**1,452**	**1,902**	**3,338**	**404**

[54]

TABLE v [continued]

ACADEMIC DEPARTMENTAL EXPENDITURE: BRITISH BUSINESS SCHOOLS, 1982/83

Institution	Departmental recurrent expenditure (£000s)						Departmental equipment expenditure
		From general income			Specific expenditure		
	Total	Salaries of academic and related staff	Other salaries and wages	Other expenditure	Research grants and contracts	Other	
Cardiff University College	171	148	12	12	–	–	4
UWIST	260	233	20	7	1	–	5
Total Wales	**431**	**380**	**32**	**19**	**1**	**–**	**9**
Total England & Wales	**12,569**	**9,804**	**1,295**	**1,471**	**1,903**	**3,339**	**413**
Edinburgh	401	340	22	39	50	26	2
Glasgow	279	233	26	20	110	–	5
Heriot-Watt	371	294	28	49	19	–	7
Stirling	261	211	36	14	–	95	6
Strathclyde	1,541	980	139	423	224	–	43
Total Scotland	**2,853**	**2,058**	**250**	**545**	**404**	**121**	**64**
Total Gt. Britain	**15,422**	**11,861**	**1,545**	**2,016**	**2,306**	**3,460**	**477**
Queen's University Belfast	191	170	18	3	23	–	2
Total N. Ireland	**191**	**170**	**18**	**3**	**23**	**–**	**2**
Total UK	**15,613**	**12,031**	**1,563**	**2,019**	**2,329**	**3,460**	**479**

Source: Universities' Statistical Record, *University Statistics 1983-84*, Vol. 6: *Finance*, Table 9 (xiv).

[55]

novel about this proposal: it would simply bring British business schools into line with the leading schools in France (INSEAD), Switzerland (IMI, IMEDE), and the United States (Harvard, Stanford, Wharton, Columbia, NYU and a host of others).

(5) *The management of the private postgraduate schools would necessarily be undertaken by their boards of directors or partners*
This arrangement would remove management from the senates and councils of the universities, for reasons lightly touched upon in the UGC's 'advice' to the Secretary of State.[1] Furthermore, the schools would be separate entities, distinct from the universities in staff funding, terms and conditions of employment, and so on.

(6) *Fundamental research would still be funded by the ESRC*
It is widely accepted that, in a market economy, 'pure' research has the characteristic of a public good. Thus the results of fundamental research are typically available to anyone and published via the academic journals. Although the private sector will not normally pay for research which has no immediate application and which it can obtain freely when published, it is clearly in the interests of society that fundamental research should be undertaken and financed.

To the extent that business schools undertake such pure research—and we are doubtful about the extent to which they do, can or should—there is a case for it to be publicly subsidised. In the UK, this would mean allowing members of staff of business schools to have access to the funding of the ESRC. Funds for applied research would continue, as now, to be sought from industry and commerce.

The financial implications of the proposals

In the absence of detailed information about individual business schools, it is difficult to estimate the precise savings to the Exchequer of our proposals. However, the orders of magnitude involved can be estimated from the figures for current expenditure from general income of UK business schools in 1982/83 of £15·6 million (Table V), with appropriate

---

[1] University Grants Committee, *A Strategy for Higher Education into the 1990s*, HMSO, September 1984, paras. 10.9, 10.11, 10.12, 10.13.

[56]

weighting for the amount spent on postgraduate provision. From this we calculate that the net recurrent grant saving is around £8 million. In 1985/86 prices, our proposals would yield a net annual saving of approximately £10 million.

We are proposing an initial government endowment to cover non-recurrent costs. The precise data necessary for calculating the size of that endowment are not available in published form and would require a more detailed analysis by the DES. For a rough order of magnitude at this stage, we have to use rough-and-ready means of calculation, which are outlined below:

—The total non-recurrent expenditure grant for all UK universities was £113·6 million in the academic year 1982/83.[1]

—Allocation of funds is to some extent based on the number of full-time students, or their equivalent.

—Since postgraduate students consume more resources than undergraduate students, it is customary to allot them a 2:1 weighting in these costs.

—Using such a weighting, the resource allocation for postgraduate non-recurrent costs in 1982/83 would have been approximately £40 million.

—UK business schools account for 5 per cent of all UK postgraduates.

On this crude reckoning, the UK business schools would require roughly £2·4 million in non-recurrent grant per year (measured at 1985-86 prices). We are seeking an initial endowment to cover £2·4 million for each of the seven years of transition. At a real discount rate of 3 per cent, the present value of £2·4 million received annually for seven years is £14·95 million. If the annual saving on the recurrent grant were £10 million per year today and were to increase in line with inflation over the next seven years, then the real discount rate should be used to evaluate the present value of the savings. This sum amounts to £62·3 million if the 3 per cent real discount rate is used. Hence the net saving over seven years, taking into account both the recurrent grant and the present cost of the annuity, is £62·3 million − £14·95 million = £47·35 million.

[1] Universities' Statistical Record, *University Statistics 1983-84*, Vol. 6, *Finance*, Table 11.

If our rough-and-ready estimates are anywhere near the mark, this figure represents quite a bargain. The size of the estimated saving would imply that, even if more precise data led to a substantial downward adjustment, the proposition would still be worth considering on economic grounds alone.

Problems of implementation

The initiation of change

Useful change is occurring within the present system but it is incremental and concentrated in areas which are largely independent of the publicly-funded cartel arrangements. For business schools to serve the national interest in any real sense, a fundamental change in ethos is required which calls for nothing less than a substantial redrawing of property rights within the schools. The initiative for such a change must come from outside the system; the obvious source is the Secretary of State for Education and Science, who would be required to relinquish his present role of funding and policing the cartel.

Time scale

The three-year transitional period suggested in this *Hobart Paper* is the academic equivalent of the Churchillian 'action this day'. British universities have many admirable qualities but prompt decision-making is not one of them. Decisions on 'run-of-the-mill' subjects go through the lengthy, cumbersome process castigated in the report of the Vice-Chancellors and Principals to the UGC (above, pp. 46-47)—and what is suggested here is no ordinary matter for decision.

Arranging for business school staff to choose between undergraduate teaching in the present UGC system or postgraduate teaching in the de-regulated system will take time, as will the transfer payments for staff employed in both undergraduate and postgraduate systems. As far as possible, this parting of the ways should take place within the first year, so that the separated staff and courses could have a two-year settling-in period before 'D-Day' (De-regulation Day).

The postgraduate schools will have to be single-minded in their attempt to produce revenue streams to offset the cessation of UGC current grant in the third year, in their negotiations with industry and commerce to build up endowment funds, in

[58]

their negotiations with government about the lump-sum endowment envisaged in this *Paper*, in the development of an integrated partnership with industry and commerce as outlined in the Franks Report, and in academic progress towards achieving the 'outreach to employers and professional bodies' sought by the UGC in its report on 'continuing education'.[1] The universities in turn will require time to adapt to the loss of their postgraduate business school activities and to integrate those members of staff of the business school who wish to transfer to undergraduate teaching.

Problems of different types of schools

There are three types of institution in business studies: predominantly postgraduate, predominantly undergraduate, and those which offer both undergraduate and postgraduate studies. Re-organisation problems are of minor significance for those schools or departments which are predominantly postgraduate or undergraduate. Those which are predominantly postgraduate—for example, the London Business School—would become de-regulated with little difficulty because their staff are on open contract and they have been preferentially and heavily endowed since their foundation, both by the Foundation for Management Education and the UGC. The predominantly undergraduate—like Leeds, Loughborough, UMIST and UWIST—would remain within the existing system with minor re-organisation problems because they have relatively little postgraduate activity.

It is with the last category which spans both undergraduate and postgraduate studies—for example, Aston, Bradford, City, Lancaster, London University and Strathclyde—that problems arise. Staff would have the option of transferring either to undergraduate courses, and thus remaining within the present system, or to the de-regulated postgraduate schools with all that entails.

If all staff opt out of postgraduate teaching in order to remain within the present system, the universities would be faced with two choices. First, they could concentrate on undergraduate business studies and attempt to attract more students to justify the numbers of transferred staff. This might be welcomed by

---

[1] University Grants Committee, *Report of the Continuing Education Working Party*, January 1984, p. 12.

the UGC which wishes to increase the proportion of vocationally-oriented courses within universities. However, while the straitjacket restriction of home student numbers remains, the increase could be achieved only at the expense of other departments within the university. Secondly, and alternatively, the universities could decide not to build up undergraduate business studies and either retrain the transferred staff or institute redundancy proceedings, preferably voluntary.

If all the staff select postgraduate studies, however, the universities would be faced with two other choices. Either they could opt out of all business studies, both undergraduate and postgraduate, and allow other departments to grow to fill the home student numbers; or they could attempt to recruit new full-time staff to replace those who had left, or to buy the services of transferred staff at commercial rates to continue to operate existing programmes.

In reality, the choice is unlikely to be as stark as that, since present business school staff would probably split between the two choices. The risk-averse or discipline-oriented would remain within the system; the risk-takers or business study-oriented would leave. The problem, albeit difficult, would therefore be manageable, and it would be achievable within the suggested time-scale.

The role of the DES, universities and business

We envisage a radical change of roles for the DES, universities and business in postgraduate studies, but no change of role in undergraduate studies. The primary role of the DES would be financial—to negotiate the terms and conditions of the endowment and to monitor the financial performance and viability of the new business schools. The primary role of the universities would be to withdraw from a sector of higher education—postgraduate business schools—into which, on our analysis, they ought not to have entered and for the running of which they are particularly ill-suited. The primary role for business would be to act in partnership with the business schools to achieve in full that 20-year-old ambition of Franks: to establish a means of increasing the 'competence of managers and those who will be managers'.

V. ARGUMENTS AGAINST THE PROPOSALS

There are typically eight arguments which are advanced against the kind of proposals we are making.

(i) *Decline in academic standards and quality*

Under a competitive market system, so the first argument goes, business schools will have an incentive to over-enrol the number of students, accept a fall in academic standards, allow an inflation of marks, and yet fail to look after the total welfare of their students. Our argument is precisely the opposite: namely, that competition will result in improved standards of teaching, more relevant curricula, and improved service for the student.

The two arguments are not necessarily in conflict. The transition from cartel to competition will certainly result in an improvement for students and in the provision of services at a lower real opportunity cost for society. Whether academic standards will decline, especially in the face of a reduction in demand in a highly competitive market, remains an open question. There is no doubt that competition will lead to more variety of quality in education—but at different prices. The more difficult issue is whether it will lead some schools to cut corners to such an extent that their students will be hurt in the process.

There remains a choice between a number of possible viewpoints. One is that standards are best protected *within* the market-place. If the market values academic standards, it will penalise any school which lets them fall too far until ultimately it goes out of business. Another viewpoint is that, if business schools are linked to existing universities for validation purposes, they have the familiar academic checks over their curricula, teaching and examination by course committees, senates and external examiners. A further approach is that business schools might establish among themselves an accreditation body, such as that developed in the United States, which would be comparable to self-regulation. The danger in the UK is that

[61]

it could easily become a backdoor substitute for the existing cartel.

(ii) *State funding is essential for higher education*

The UGC has stated its belief that 'any government which looked for a major change in the balance between public and private funding of universities would be deceiving itself...'.[1] It quotes the CBI with approval:

> 'The state must continue to support higher education. It cannot opt out. It is unrealistic to expect anything more than marginal funding from business, which is after all only one of the users of the higher education system.'[2]

The UGC was here reviewing the whole spectrum of university activities, across all departments, both graduate and undergraduate. It may be unrealistic to expect a major change from public to private funding of the whole of higher education to take place in the immediate future. It is a judgement we respect. But it is wrong to infer that, because market funding is thought to be inapplicable to most university activities, it must therefore be ruled out for *every* university activity. Indeed, the UGC partly recognised this *non sequitur*:

> '*We see advantages, however, in an increase in the number of postgraduate students who are not financed from public funds.* Some taught courses provide advanced and post-experience education of direct and immediate benefit to industry and commerce. The contribution which students from such courses can make is recognised in the high financial rewards available to them. Many of the students already pay their own fees and maintenance costs. *We believe that the public interest would be well served if more students were encouraged to follow their example.* The wider availability of commercial loan schemes to assist students with these costs would be a very valuable addition to the present public support arrangements...'.[3]

Despite the logic of this statement, the UGC shrinks from accepting it fully. Whilst encouraging the market mechanism and welcoming a commercial loan scheme for students, it sees both as merely a 'valuable addition to the present public support arrangements'. The idea that they might supplant and replace

[1] University Grants Committee, *A Strategy ...*, *op. cit.*, para. 9.4.
[2] *Ibid.*, para. 9.5.
[3] *Ibid.*, para. 9.24 (italics added).

the 'public support arrangements', even for postgraduate education, is plainly rejected. The entire section 9 of the UGC's *Strategy* report is based on the assumption that universities have a right to public support.[1]

(iii) *Discrimination against management training*

Our view is that *all* vocational postgraduate training should be privately rather than publicly funded. Why should management education be the only sector to benefit by liberation from the academic stranglehold? Postgraduate education is generally sought by students as a means of equipping themselves the better to pursue a particular career and of enhancing their promotion prospects. The training enables them to earn higher salaries and make a bigger contribution to the companies or institutions they join. This logic applies to a whole range of postgraduate courses, from engineering, medicine and veterinary science to those in the arts and law.

The management education sector should be considered the primary candidate for a change from public to private funding, first, because the case for such a change can be most clearly seen here in familiar economic terms, and, second, because it would provide a useful model for other areas of vocational postgraduate training to follow.

(iv) *Externalities in higher education*

If it is true that higher education yields externalities, this is an extremely important objection to our proposals. A sophisticated formulation of this argument has been provided by Professor Sir James Ball, a former Principal of the London Business School:

'There has never been any dispute about the fact that the financing of continuing education in management should fall on individual participants and participating companies. And so it has been the case. The only issue in contention is state support for postgraduate education and presumably also for undergraduate education in business and management studies. The suggestion that support for postgraduate education in management should fall on individual companies while the state continues to support the education of doctors, accountants and engineers,

[1] *A Strategy* . . ., paras. 9.4, 9.5, 9.6, 9.7, 9.18, 9.20, 9.21, 9.23 and 9.24.

[63]

seems to me to reflect, in the first place, an extraordinary intellectual error and, in the second place, an equally extraordinary ignorance of what has been happening in British industry over the last 30 years.

The first error arises from the simple classical economic consideration that, whereas continuing education is legitimately financed by participating companies upon whom the direct benefits may be reasonably expected to fall, the externalities of graduate activities are such as to make it quite clear that the social benefits of graduate education (insofar as there are benefits) are likely to exceed the possible benefits to any one company, so justifying in a classical economic liberal sense the case for subsidy and state support.'[1]

The claim here is that the marginal *social* benefit from postgraduate business education is larger than the marginal *private* benefit to an individual or to a company (if the individual is financed by the company). This implies that, in a free market in which individuals based their decisions on their private returns, student enrolment at business schools would fall and the total number of business school graduates would be less than the social optimum.

For education in basic literacy and numeracy, there is an obvious case for the existence of externalities and for a state subsidy. But for postgraduate business education, where the returns from the investment are captured in a competitive market by the individuals concerned, it is difficult to imagine what kind of externalities there can be. Although Professor Ball makes a strong plea for a state subsidy, he does not specify the externalities which may exist. Additionally, he draws a sharp distinction between postgraduate education in management and post-experience training. It is precisely this sharp separation which we find difficult to justify intellectually.

In its recent *Strategy* report to the Secretary of State for Education and Science, the UGC sees advantages in increasing the number of postgraduate students who are not financed from public funds. And it goes on to observe:

'Some *taught* courses provide advanced and post-experience education of direct and immediate value to industry and commerce. The contribution which students from such courses can make is recognised in the high financial rewards available to them.

[1] Sir James Ball, Second Stockton Lecture, *Management Education in the UK*, London Business School, February 1983.

[64]

Many of the students already pay their own fees and maintenance costs. We believe that the public interest would be well served if more students were encouraged to follow their example' (para. 9.24).

This is hardly an argument which could be based on the evidence of substantial externalities. Even if externalities did exist, however, they would still establish only a *potential* case for a state subsidy. It would have to be shown that they were of a sufficient size to outweigh the costs involved in channelling the same funds through the public sector. The present system is far from costless!

A further fallacy linked to this objection goes something as follows: The price charged to a student at Harvard University is less than half of the real cost; the student is subsidised from the endowment provided by Harvard alumni; in Britain this endowment is state provided out of taxation; subsidy is necessary from whatever source; and that necessity proves there are externalities . . .

The fallacy here lies in the argument that, because in certain countries state subsidies are given to postgraduate business schools, and because private universities with postgraduate business schools are supported by private endowments, it therefore follows that externalities must exist. But the fact that an industry enjoys state or private subsidies is neither a necessary nor a sufficient condition to demonstrate the existence of externalities. Subsidies do not imply externalities. Once again, we are forced to challenge those who use this argument for state support so passionately to produce tangible evidence of the existence of such externalities in the UK.

There is yet another twist to the externalities argument. Individual companies may benefit by recruiting graduates whose training has been financed by others. To benefit from such recruitment the company must perceive a difference between private and social cost. This implies the existence of externalities. Contrary to what is claimed, the initial proposition in this statement is not at all obvious. If an MBA course increases the value of human capital embodied in the graduating student, this will be reflected in the market-place by a higher salary for the individual concerned. The course may have been financed by the individual, a corporation, a charity, the state, or some combination of them. The source of finance is hardly relevant to the potential employer who has to pay the higher

[65]

salary associated with recruiting an MBA graduate. There is no sense in which that employer gains at someone else's expense. If he were to hire an MBA graduate whose course had been financed by a company which had previously employed him, the graduate would be the gainer and his former company the loser. But this simply demonstrates the redistribution involved and has nothing whatever to do with externalities.

(v) *Distortions of staff time*

It is sometimes contended that increased private funding would lead to a distortion of staff time.

> '. . . the search by universities for additional income for services rendered incurs substantial administrative costs and makes considerable demands on the time of senior academic staff. There must be a point at which the benefit of securing extra income is outweighed by the loss to non-commercial teaching and research.'[1]

This kind of criticism must be seen in the context of the present system, where the UGC itself is quite outspoken about the staff time which universities spend on deciding the allocation of resources by committees rather than markets. The change we recommend will be an unambiguous improvement over the present system for everyone—except those who have invested time and effort to develop the skills appropriate to the internal bureaucracy of modern universities.

In a competitive system there would be *no* distortion to staff time: those who were skilled at teaching would teach, those who were skilled at research would research, and those who were skilled at management would in practice manage the schools whose creation we advocate. This system works extremely well in private American universities.[2]

(vi) *Distribution of income leads to capital market 'failure'*

Another argument is that potential students from differing income backgrounds would have varying access to the schools. Thus students from a working-class background would be at a disadvantage in comparison with those from a high-income

---

[1] UGC, *A Strategy* . . ., *op. cit.*, para. 9.4.

[2] It could be argued that diseconomies might result from the very small scale of most UK business schools. A normal business solution to this problem is merger.

one; they would be less able to afford postgraduate business education because they would be less able to borrow from the financial institutions.

The relevance of this argument for postgraduate business education seems to us very slight indeed. The collateral against which any individual can borrow is his income-earning potential; and a career in business is good collateral. Our experience, in those cases in which students require loan finance, is that acceptance by a business school for a postgraduate course is normally a sufficient guarantee for a bank to advance a loan. If for some reason there was a capital market failure, there would be an argument on public policy grounds for increased competition in that part of the credit market and for government to permit more institutions to make that kind of loan. In the worst possible case—which we cannot imagine developing—the government could step in and guarantee the loan.

We would emphasise, however, that an efficient capital market for student loans does not mean that every student who applies for a loan to cover the full cost of fees and maintenance is likely to be awarded one. It may be that some potential students reveal themselves to be poor risks or, even worse, poor investments. But a system which appraises future earning power in this way could in no derogatory sense be called discriminatory.

(vii) *Consumer ignorance*

There is a well-worn argument that, because individuals do not have sufficient knowledge to make proper choices, their decisions will result in an inefficient allocation of resources. There is less chance of that happening under a reformed structure since the producers themselves (the business schools) would be under considerable market pressure to inform potential students of the value of their courses.

(viii) *The politicised alternative*

The most extreme criticism of our proposals would be the advocacy of more government involvement in higher education—including, we would presume, business education. Such an approach has been advocated by Mr Peter Scott, the editor of *The Times Higher Education Supplement*:

'. . . in the end the best way to stimulate change may be to accept a strong political presence in the making of Higher Education policy . . . After all, it is only within the context of closer political involvement that issues like modification of tenure, reform of student support . . . and other policies that are regarded as central to the process of change can be effectively tackled . . . Nor should closer political involvement be seen as a threat to the autonomy and integrity of Higher Education. *There is a strong case for arguing that the state can protect Higher Education from the more immediate pressures of the market-place, very much as the establishment of the UGC and the consolidation of a reliable system of government grants to universities in fact insulated universities from the crude pressures of industrial sponsors and fee-paying students.*'[1]

This political involvement—continuous, not once-for-all—would be effected, directed and controlled by what Scott called

'the steady accumulation of power at the centre, in the DES and in national agencies like the UGC and the NAB. Within institutions a similar concentration of power over allocation of resources is also likely . . .'.[2]

It is remarkable that this tight political control, with its ever-increasing centralisation of power, is considered preferable to control by consumers. We doubt whether most staff or students would regard market orientation as so abhorrent that they would prefer centralised bureaucratic control.

Scott's crude arguments against market orientation are scarcely persuasive. Suggesting that higher education is a commodity in short supply and likely to remain so while it consumes a large public subsidy, he argues that 'voucher' or 'loan' schemes would have no significant effect on total supply. Access would, therefore, be politically determined and the market would be 'contrived'. But we are proposing a *withdrawal* of state funding, so that lack of public finance would no longer act as a constraint on supply. We advocate an 'open-ended' market and reject Scott's suggestion that this would not be 'desirable in terms of academic and professional standards and values'.

It is Scott's inability to envisage a significant withdrawal of public funds and their substitution by private funding that vitiates his argument. It says a great deal for the persuasive

[1] Peter Scott, *The Crisis of the University*, Croom Helm, 1984, p. 69 (italics added).
[2] Peter Scott, *ibid.*, p. 70.

force of the present cartel that its continued existence should have such an unquestioned axiomatic hold over those within and outside the system. We find it astonishing that direction by an inner cabal of politicians, bureaucrats and administrators could be considered obviously superior to the influence exerted by users and consumers of higher education.

VI. THE WAY FORWARD

Implications of the reform plan

One result of our reforms would be an annual financial saving to the Treasury of something around £10 million. This would be made up of the costs of salaries, equipment, rent and rates and other administrative charges, as well as student awards made by the ESRC. To the extent that the financing of business schools would be transferred from the taxpayer to companies and students, reform would represent only a marginal improvement to society through lower taxes. Its real social benefits would come from a number of other sources:

(a) an improvement in the efficiency (defined in terms of Leibenstein's X-efficiency concept) with which business schools are run;

(b) increased competition through the removal of the cartel;

(c) the changing nature of the service provided by business schools to their students and the business community; and

(d) a more dynamic responsiveness by business schools to changing market conditions.

Implicit in all these benefits is the effect they would have on the internal management of business schools. A market discipline would be introduced with the result that badly-managed schools would risk going out of business. This prospect would act as a powerful incentive to focus the minds of those in business schools on ensuring that their product mix, its quality, design and price were attractive, and that they had a professional marketing strategy.

Another implication of the reform plan is the effect it would have on the terms and conditions of employment at the new schools. Tenure would be abolished in favour of fixed-term contracts varying in length, some perhaps continuing up to retirement where institutions wished to retain particular staff.

[70]

Tenure, however, would not be the norm or general expectation. As for salaries, we would expect to see a general increase —thereby narrowing the differential between teaching at business school and being employed in business. We would also expect much wider variations in remuneration than among present business school staff. We would expect business schools to remunerate staff on the basis of their varying contribution to the profitability of the institution. Salaries would be fixed by the management of the new schools with individual members of staff.

A third impact would be on teaching and the quality of service received by students. Since schools would be competing directly against each other on price, they would be forced by market pressure to make sure that their teaching was first-rate. Staff would be paid to be good teachers. They would also be paid to ensure that the total teaching package they delivered— in terms of presentation, visual aids, lecture notes—was of the highest standard. If the teaching was less than first-rate, institutions would suffer and, in the extreme, go to the wall.

A fourth effect of these reforms is the impact they would have on the number of students qualifying with management training. Because the training programmes would be much more closely tailored to the requirements of individual companies, and because schools would possess the finance to hire first-class teachers, we believe it would lead to a significant increase in the number of UK students training at UK business schools, and enable UK business schools to make considerable inroads into the growing world market in business education.

A final result is the example it would set to other postgraduate vocational education, and especially engineering. The de-regulation of business schools should be seen as a first step towards the de-regulation of all postgraduate vocational training in British universities.

Intellectual but practical

We have accepted the judgement of business that business schools are too 'academic' and 'not practical' enough in the training they offer. To avoid being misunderstood by our academic colleagues, it is important that we clarify these terms and others, since they are sometimes used in a loose way.

We believe that business schools should have the highest

[71]

intellectual standards. By this we mean that courses should be taught with an emphasis on analytical rigour, that they should be oriented to problem-solving, and that they should use and develop skills of literacy, numeracy and computing. We also believe that business schools should be at the frontiers of knowledge in order to help business formulate successful strategies in a rapidly changing environment—which entails substantial research. If this is what is meant by the expression 'academic' as applied to business schools, then business schools should most certainly be academic.

But we also believe that the subjects taught in business schools should be relevant to business practice. For example, economics should be related to the concerns of business management, not of a potential Treasury official or academic economist. Similarly, pyschology and sociology should be integrated into courses on the management of human resources, rather than being taught as intellectual disciplines in their own right. Relevance, in our judgement, does not mean sloppy intellectual standards or a bias against the teaching of theory. But that theory must be useful to future managers. The temptation facing academics in business schools is to err in the direction of playing with theoretical models for their own sake and for publication in academic journals rather than developing them in the service of business.

Integration with the market

The new business schools, as joint academic/business partnerships, would be orientated towards analysing and then meeting the needs of their customers in industry and commerce. They would meet not only the initial education and training requirements of staff but also the continuing educational demands caused by changes in technology and in social and economic conditions. As the UGC observed in 1984:

'Apart from the updating of existing skills . . . as the demands of management roles and the need for business awareness in technical roles increase, it becomes necessary to acquire new skills.'[1]

In the USA, there is close involvement of business schools

[1] University Grants Committee, *Continuing Education Working Party, op. cit.,* Appendix II.

in industrial and commercial training. In the UK, many 'assist some public and private sector employers with their in-house training programmes. . . . But the total involvement remains very small'.[1] The UGC Working Party went on to urge that this be developed further to the advantage of both parties:

'It would lead to a strong association between a core of employers and the university and thus lessen the distinction between those who teach and those who practice a profession. Also the involvement of experienced and knowledgeable employees in the teaching process is a very effective way of ensuring that courses remain up-to-date and relevant. Such links have benefitted the medical profession in the UK and engineers in Germany and the US, where employees move with relative ease between industry and educational institutions' (para. 36).

This 'forward integration' to the market-place, and ease of interchange of academic and business staff, cannot be effected within the present structure, however much the Working Party on Continuing Education may wish and urge it. For reasons already outlined, only the new structure can achieve it.

What is required is not just an extension of post-experience courses, with the venue varied between campus and company. A whole-hearted integration of industrial and commercial training under the aegis of a business school is essential. In other words, company in-house courses would be brought into the business school 'out-reach' programme. The entire career development, education and training programmes of particular firms, within chosen commercial sectors, in the immediate catchment areas of each business school would be designed, developed and taught co-operatively by company staff and business school academics. And, where desired, courses would be validated as modular components of educational qualifications such as diplomas, MBAs and DBAs. Business schools alone cannot supply the total educational and training package required by industrial and commercial companies; they have no monopoly on course design, content or teaching skills. What the new business schools could do, however, is to develop a co-ordinating role, integrating commercial and industrial training into a complete educational structure. This is a newly perceived intellectual and practical challenge and business school staff have the capability to meet it.

[1] *Ibid.*, p. 12, para. 36.

[73]

The role of business

The role of business in the new schools would no longer be as a passive recipient of business school offerings. It would play a joint role in determining the strategy of business schools and the allocation of resources within them. It would encourage the integration of business and business school activity at all levels within the chosen sectors of commercial and industrial specialisation. It would help develop new courses to anticipate new demands or more effectively meet existing ones, and help develop relevant teaching material and ensure it remained up-to-date. It would facilitate the movement of business school staff into industry and commerce to gain experience of day-to-day management problems, and of business staff into the business school to gain experience of course planning, research and teaching.

This role for business is in line with that indicated by the UGC Working Party on Continuing Education which, given the present structures, could suggest only minor improvements. We suggest removing the constraints and so transforming the prospects for continuing education.

For smaller companies in the chosen sectors, whose capacity for in-house training is limited, the business school would develop, in partnership, a whole range of education and training programmes—to be mounted both on campus and on site.

Curricula/course development

Implicitly, we would expect business schools to specialise in those market segments in which they had comparative advantages of location and quality of staff. The market segments would reflect and determine the strategy of a school as it sought to identify ever more closely with the industrial/commercial sector it aimed to serve. Each school would strive *not* to produce generalised courses or generalised students; it would not seek to be all things to all men.

The specialisation of business schools in particular sectors of the economy would permit: more concentration of research activity; the co-operative application of that research to decision-making; the provision of relevant teaching material, examples, case histories and studies; the building up of in-depth knowledge and experience among teaching staff; much more exposure to that research and teaching throughout the chosen

[74]

sectors; and the monitoring of course/teaching effectiveness in terms of improved performance.

What we are seeking above all is not more of the same but a radical transformation of course and curriculum development, as well as of teaching and research methodology.

It is inherent in the proposed integration of business schools and company training programmes that the opportunities for research within those companies would be enhanced and that research would be business-oriented and *not* discipline-oriented. Such an approach has been termed 'pop research' by some business school academics, implying that only research within an academic discipline has intellectual rigour. This would mean that only topics of little direct relevance to business are worthy of the term scholarship! Research in the business schools must have an objective—that of facilitating the improvement of managerial competence. Anything else is self-indulgence on the part of the researcher.

*   *   *

This analysis will not meet with the unanimous approval of our colleagues in the business schools. Many will seek to explain away the relative failure to satisfy expectations. Others will accept the case for change but argue for a gradualist approach which preserves total job security.

There are those who think our analysis is not a problem to be minimised or explained away, but rather an opportunity to be taken boldly. We are of like mind with them.

VII. SUMMARY AND CONCLUSIONS

1. We are convinced that rigorous postgraduate and post-experience business education has a major contribution to make to the creation of wealth in the United Kingdom and that business schools could play a more important role in this process.

2. The present system suffers from crucial weaknesses: it is too academic in the traditional sense of that term, it is hedged about with far too many restrictions, and it is too remote from business.

3. These weaknesses can be traced not just to the fact that Franks's views were only partially implemented but also to the fundamental flaws in the original conception of business schools as still substantially publicly-funded and part of an industry which suffers from being organised as a classic cartel.

4. Modest change can be achieved within the present system. But the potential which business schools have for furthering the interests of the nation will never be realised without a formal break from government control and funding.

5. The first requirement for radical reform is to separate undergraduate business education from postgraduate business education—which would be taught in postgraduate business schools with the status of independent legal entities outside the public sector.

6. Over a three-year period, all postgraduate business school activtiy would cease to be government-funded and would be financed by fees and endowments.

7. Salaries and terms and conditions of employment at the private postgraduate business schools would be market-determined; the schools would be managed by their boards of directors or partners.

[76]

8. Because fundamental research is a public good which yields benefits not confined to its initiators, it would continue to be funded by the ESRC.

9. We believe that students, business, business schools and government would all benefit from the de-regulation we advocate. Students would receive higher standards of teaching and service; the business schools would find themselves with an enlarged market and rationale (or, in strictly economic terms, an increase in their net wealth); and business would find itself more actively involved in the training process and better served; and government would be enabled to reduce its expenditure.

10. Removing government controls and funding from business schools should not be seen as an end in itself. It should be implemented as an example of the way in which all vocational postgraduate education could be transferred to the private sector, with an improvement in the quality and diversity of training, and much larger eventual reductions in support by taxpayers.

BIBLIOGRAPHY

Ascher, Kate, *Masters of Business: the MBA and British industry*, Harbridge House Europe, 1984.

Ball, R. J., 'Management Education in the United Kingdom', Second Stockton Lecture, delivered on 10 February 1983, published in *London Business School Journal*, Summer 1983.

Barron, Sir Donald, 'Management Education—Theory and Practice', First Stockton Lecture, delivered on 13 January 1983, published in *London Business School Journal*, Summer 1983.

British Institute of Management, *The employment of graduates*, BIM, London, 1968.

——, *Management education in the 1970s*, Proceedings of the Management Education Review Conference, British Institute of Management, London, 1970.

——, *Business school programmes: the requirements of British manufacturing industry* (The Owen Report), British Institute of Management, London, 1971.

——, *National management salary survey*, British Institute of Management, London, 1977.

——, *Industry, education and management*, Report of a BIM Working Party, British Institute of Management, London, 1979.

The Business Graduate, Special Issue, 'Management Education in the 1980s', Winter 1979.

Business Graduates Association, *Business graduates: some attitudes towards business schools*, BGA, 1976.

——, *British industry's attitude to business graduates and business schools*, BGA, 1971.

——, *Business school education in the 1980s: an agenda for discussion*, BGA, Spring 1982.

——, *Higher management education and the production function*, BGA, November 1977.

[78]

Committee of Vice-Chancellors and Principals, *Annual Report 1983-84*, September 1984.

——, Steering Committee for Efficiency Studies in Universities, *National Data Study*, published in association with Coopers & Lybrand Associates, March 1985.

——, *Report of the Steering Committee for Efficiency Studies in Universities* (The Jarratt Report), March 1985.

——, & University Grants Committee, *Tuition Fees: Final Report of a Joint Working Party*, June 1976.

Crew, Michael, and Young, Alistair, *Paying by Degrees*, Hobart Paper 75, Institute of Economic Affairs, 1977.

Education, Science and Arts Committee, Fifth Report, Session 1979-80, *The Funding and Organisation of Courses in Higher Education: Volume I: Minutes of Evidence*, HMSO, 4 June 1980.

Education, Science and Arts Committee, Fifth Report, Session 1979-80, *The Funding and Organisation of Courses in Higher Education: Volume II: Minutes of Evidence*, HMSO, 12 September 1980.

Expenditure Committee, Third Report, together with the minutes of the evidence taken before the Education and Arts Sub-Committee in Session 1972-73, Appendices and Index, Session 1973-74, *Postgraduate Education: Volume I: Report*, HMSO, 20 December 1973.

Forrester, Peter, *A study of the practical use of the MBA*, British Institute of Management, 1984.

Foy, Nancy, *The missing links: British management education in the eighties*, Oxford Centre for Management Studies, September 1978.

Franks, Lord, *British Business Schools*, British Institute of Management, 1963.

Gordon, Alan, Hutt, Rosemary, and Pearson, Richard, *Undergraduate Sponsorship: Implications for the Labour Market*, Interim Report to the Leverhulme Trust, IMS Report No. 82, Institute of Manpower Studies, January 1984.

Hall, Sir Noel, *Academic Freedom in Management Education*, The Second Urwick Lecture, British Institute of Management, January 1966.

Handy, C. B., 'Business schools—missionaries or mercenaries?', *International Management Development*, 1977.

Henley Conference Report, 'The Future of Management Schools', *The Business Graduate*, May 1983.

[79]

Hofstede, G., 'Businessmen and business school faculty: a comparison of value systems', *Journal of Management Studies*, 1978.

Kogan, Maurice, and Kogan, David, *The attack on higher education*, Kogan Page, 1983.

Leavitt, Harold J., 'Management and Management Education in the West: what's right and what's wrong', Third Stockton Lecture, delivered on 16 March 1983, published in *London Business School Journal*, Summer 1983.

Lewis, Alan, Sandford, Cedric, and Thomson, Norman, *Grants or Loans?*, Research Monograph 34, Institute of Economic Affairs, 1980.

Lupton, T. 'Business education, British style', *Newsletter*, Centre for Business Research, Manchester Business School, Spring 1972.

Mant, Alistair, *The Experienced Manager: a major resource*, British Institute of Management, 1969.

Maynard, Alan, *Experiment with Choice in Education*, Hobart Paper 64, Institute of Economic Affairs, 1975.

Morris, Alfred, and Sizer, John, *Resources and Higher Education*, Leverhulme Programme of Study into the Future of Higher Education, 1982.

Partridge, Sir John, 'What's wrong with business education?', *The Economist*, 21 November 1970.

Pearson, Richard (ed.), *Industry and higher education: future collaboration*, IMS Report No. 79, Institute of Manpower Studies jointly with *The Times Higher Education Supplement*, 1983.

Peel, Malcolm, *Management Development and Training: a survey of current policy*, British Institute of Management, 1984.

European Foundation for Management Development, Report of the Committee on *Educational and training needs of European managers* (Pocock Report), EFMD, 1977.

Robbins, Lord (Chairman), Committee on Higher Education, *Higher Education: Report*, Cmnd. 2154, HMSO, 1963.

——, Committee on Higher Education, *Higher Education: Appendix Four: Administrative, Financial and Economic Aspects of Higher Education*, Cmnd. 2154-IV, HMSO, 1963.

Robertson, Andrew, and others, 'Business Schools: Is the Backlash Justified?', *Management Decision*, Autumn 1970.

Roscoe, John, *The Diploma in Management Studies: a survey*, British Institute of Management, London, 1975.

Rose, H. R., *Management education in the 70s: growth and issues*, HMSO, London, 1970.

Select Committee on Science and Technology, The Government's Reply to the Third Report, Session 1975-76, *University-Industry Relations*, Cmnd. 6928, HMSO, September 1977.

Sizer, John, *Performance assessment in non-profit organisations: the case of higher education under conditions of financial stringency and changing needs*, ICMA Occasional Papers Series, Institute of Cost and Management Accountants, 1981.

Touche Ross Report on *Business education*, Touche Ross, 1984.

The University Grants Committee, *Annual Survey, Academic Year 1965-66 and Review of University Development 1962-63 to 1965-66*, Cmnd. 3192, HMSO, February 1967.

——, *Annual Survey, Academic Year 1979-80*, Cmnd. 8359, September 1981.

——, *Annual Survey, Academic Year 1981-82*, Cmnd. 8965, HMSO, July 1983.

——, *Annual Survey, Academic Year 1982-83*, Cmnd. 9234, HMSO, May 1984.

——, *Returns from Universities and University Colleges in receipt of Exchequer Grant: Academic year 1964-1965*, Cmnd. 3106, HMSO, October 1966.

——, *A Strategy for Higher Education into the 1990s*, HMSO, September 1984.

——, *University Development, 1947-52*, Cmd. 8875, HMSO, July 1953.

——, *University Development, 1957-62*, Cmnd. 2267, HMSO, February 1964.

——, *University Development, 1962-67*, Cmnd. 3820, HMSO, November 1968.

——, *University Development, 1967-72*, Cmnd. 5728, HMSO, September 1974.

Universities' Statistical Record, *University Statistics 1983-84*, Vol. 1, *Students and Staff*, USR on behalf of the UGC, October 1984.

Universities' Statistical Record, *University Statistics 1983-84*, Vol. 6, *Finance*, USR on behalf of the UGC, October 1984.

Whitley, R. D., and Thomas, A. B., 'A new business elite: the background and early careers of business school graduates', *Manchester Business School Review*, 1980.

Whitley, R. B., Thomas, A. B., and Marceau, Jane, *Masters of Business? Business schools and business graduates in Britain and France*, Tavistock Studies in Sociology, 1981.

Wills, Gordon, *Business School Graffiti: a decennial transcript*, MCB Books, 1976.

Woodhall, Maurice, *Student Loans: Lessons from recent international experience*, PSI, May 1982.

Working Group on the Management of Higher Education in the Maintained Sector, *Report*, Cmnd. 7130, HMSO, March 1978.

TOPICS FOR DISCUSSION

1. What are the various externalities of business school education that justify taxpayers' support? Suggest how they may be measured.

2. What would be the effect on the performance of British universities if:

   (a) public funding was substantially reduced but the cartel maintained;

   (b) the cartel was abolished but the public funding maintained?

3. Who are the customers which British business schools seek to serve?

4. In which ways would the argument for tenured employment differ in the cases of: (i) coal miners, (ii) professional footballers, (iii) bankers, (iv) university staff, (v) taxi drivers?

5. Imagine British business schools formed an Accreditation Body. Using the modern theory of bureaucracy, what predictions would you make about the policy such a body would adopt?

6. Is the distaste for the market-place manifested by British universities a cause or effect of the UK's relative economic decline?

7. 'Throughout the world business education is subsidised, either directly by the state or through charitable donations.' Discuss.

8. If all public funding was withdrawn from postgraduate business education in the UK, what would you expect to be the likely effects on: (i) the total number of schools established in the UK; (ii) the range of courses offered; (iii) the

range of prices for a standard MBA degree course; and (iv) the corporate strategies of different schools?

9. Discuss the pros and cons of business schools being established as limited liability companies.

10. Is academic freedom under more severe threat from public funding than from private funding?

Some IEA Books on Education

Education and the State
E. G. WEST
1965   Second Edition 1971   Hard Cover £2·50   Paperback £1·25
'. . . perhaps the most important work written on the subject this
century.'   *Sunday Times*
'A piece of intellectual dynamite.'   *Sunday Telegraph*

Hobart Paper 25
Education for Democrats
ALAN T. PEACOCK and JACK WISEMAN
1964   Second Impression 1970
'. . . what the authors of this booklet want is a free market in
education, with people (usually using vouchers, grants or loans from
the state) shopping around for the education they like.'
                                                          Yorkshire Post

IEA Readings 1
Education: A Framework for Choice
A. C. F. BEALES, MARK BLAUG, E. G. WEST,
DOUGLAS VEALE
1967   xvi + 100pp.   Second Edition 1970   £1·00
'The more the voucher scheme is discussed the clearer it becomes
that it would be quite feasible to draw up a scheme, and that the
small print on the back of the voucher could provide for any number
of different interpretations.'   *Education*

Hobart Paper 42
Economics, Education and the Politician
E. G. WEST
1968   Second Impression 1976   £1·00
'. . . marshals some alarming statistics to emphasise the need for a
modification of the financing of the primary schools.'
                                          The Times Educational Supplement

Hobart Paper 64
Experiment with Choice in Education
ALAN MAYNARD
1975   £1·00
'Alan Maynard again argues the case for educational vouchers and
calls for practical experiments. His appeal deserves serious
consideration.'   *The Times*, in an Editorial

Hobart Paper 75
Paying by Degrees
MICHAEL A. CREW and ALISTAIR YOUNG
1977   Out of print

Occasional Paper 12
Financing University Education
A. R. PREST
1966   50p
'. . . Professor Prest has refined some of the practical details of his loan system. His broad idea is that a loan scheme could be devised for repayments to vary with income . . .'
                                        The Times Educational Supplement

Occasional Paper 25
Towards an Independent University
H. S. FERNS
1969   Second Edition 1970   50p
'The proposals for an independent university outside the state-financed system set out by Professor Ferns may appear utopian and impractical, yet they deserve careful study.'
                                        Glasgow Herald, in an Editorial

Research Monograph 34
Grants or Loans?
ALAN LEWIS, CEDRIC SANDFORD, NORMAN THOMSON
1980   £2·00
'British students should pay their own way through college or university—with the help of loans, according to a new survey . . . And the expensive multi-million pound system of handing out undergraduates' state grants must be abolished, say two out of three members of the public.'   *Evening Standard*

Occasional Paper 65
How Much Freedom for Universities?
H. S. FERNS
With an Economic Commentary by JOHN BURTON
1982   £1·50
'State funding of universities . . . should be phased out. Instead universities, polytechnics and colleges should become independent companies free to sell whatever courses they like for whatever price they can command.'   *The Observer*

Hobart Paperback 19
Choice in Education
An analysis of the political economy of state and private education
S. R. DENNISON
1984   xii + 96pp.   £2·50
'Perhaps teachers should pay heed to Professor Dennison . . . who has discovered that cuts don't matter as there is no correlation between expenditure and the academic results which he takes to be the sole criterion of educational success.'
                                        The Times Educational Supplement

Some recent IEA publications

Hobart Paperback 20

Farming for Farmers?

A critique of agricultural support policy

Richard Howarth   1985   xvi + 144 pp.   £4·00

'Richard Howarth argues with a wealth of supporting evidence that the withering away of the Common Agricultural Policy would not only serve the interests of consumers, but also do no great harm to the majority of producers.' J. Bruce-Gardyne, *Sunday Telegraph*

'Mr Howarth shows a grasp of the real world of farming and the Common Agriculture Policy. His suggestion that the CAP should be allowed, and encouraged, to continue the withering-away process and his ideas on the equivalent of redundancy payments for miners or steelworkers are . . . well thought out.'   *Big Farm Weekly*

Occasional Paper 71

No, Minister!

A radical challenge on economic and social policies from speeches in the House of Lords

Ralph Harris   1985   £1·80

'. . . debates a measure in Britain's House of Lords calling for more equality.'   *Wall Street Journal* (Brussels)

Occasional Paper 72

Wage-Fixing Revisited

A revised and expanded text of the fourth Robbins Lecture

J. E. Meade   1985   £1·50

'The Institute of Economic Affairs has chosen a timely moment to publish Professor James Meade's paper . . . Professor Meade, winner of the Nobel prize for economics in 1977 and one of the authors of the 1944 White Paper on employment policy addresses a familiar theme. Wage determination is the central problem facing democratic economies and, without a radical change in the system of wage-fixing in Britain, the alleviation of unemployment will only be achieved at the expense of far higher inflation.'

The Times, in an Editorial

Research Monograph 39

Competition and Home Medicines

W. Duncan Reekie
and
Hans G. Ötzbrugger   1985   £1·80

economic affairs

A quarterly journal of economic analysis and commentary, published by Longman Group Limited in association with the Institute of Economic Affairs

Editor: Arthur Seldon

Economic Affairs is topical, readable and provocative. It provides economists with a forum to discuss recent, current and impending developments, allowing them to respond quickly to new trends and events.

In concise, non-technical language authors challenge accepted wisdom. Using both micro- and macro-economic methods, they shed light on traditional economic subjects and extend the use of economic analysis to a host of new occupations, services, products and industries.

Economic Affairs is read in 50 countries, by economists, government officials, businessmen, labour leaders, academics, teachers and students who need to keep up-to-date with current thinking.

Since 1980, **Economic Affairs** has published the work of over 250 authors from the UK and overseas, including:

Norman Barry – Michael Beenstock – Roy Batchelor – Mark Blaug – Alan Budd – Karl Brunner – John Burton – Frank Chapple – Anthony Christopher – Tim Congdon – Stanley Dennison – Walter Eltis – Edgar Feige – Herbert Giersch – David Green – Jo Grimond – Ralph Harris – F. A. Hayek – David Henderson – Sir Geoffrey Howe – Richard Jackman – Israel Kirzner – David Laidler – Stephen Littlechild – Allan Meltzer – Patrick Minford – Mancur Olson – David Owen – Kristian Palda – Alan Peacock – Lord Robbins – Colin Robinson – Anna Schwartz – Ljubo Sirc – Gordon Tullock – Roland Vaubel – E. G. West – Geoffrey Wood – Basil Yamey.

Economic Affairs   ISSN 0265-0665
published quarterly, in October, January, April and July.

For subscription details, please write to:

LONGMAN GROUP LTD.
Subscriptions Department (Journals),
Fourth Avenue, Harlow, Essex CM19 5AA, England.